CHILDREN'S GUIDE TO THE
HUMAN BODY

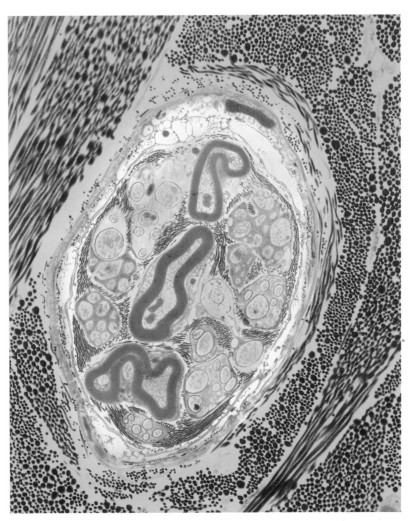

A cross-section through a nerve in the skin

CHILDREN'S GUIDE TO THE
HUMAN BODY

DR. NAOMI CRAFT

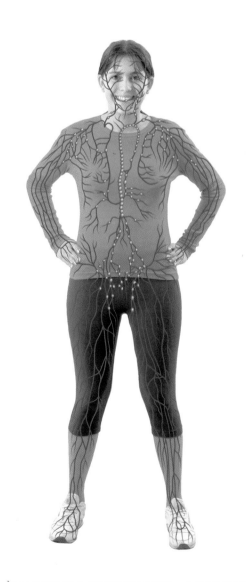

MARSHALL PUBLISHING • LONDON

Rod and cone cells in the retina of the eye

A Marshall Edition
Conceived, edited and designed by
Marshall Editions Ltd
The Orangery
161 New Bond Street
London W1S 2UF
www.marshallpublishing.com

First published in the UK in 2001 by
Marshall Publishing Ltd

ISBN 1 84028 446 3

The author would like to thank Natasha and Isaac Hyman
for providing her with inspiration.

Consultants: Dr. Abi Berger, Paula Messam MSc,
    Dr. Deanna D'Souza
Managing Editor: Janet Sacks
Design Manager: Ralph Pitchford
Editorial Manager: Kate Phelps
Editors: Caroline Greene, Robert Dinwiddie
Additional editorial assistance: Vanessa Morgan
Designers: Ed Simkins, Judith Bussmann
Picture Researcher: Andrea Sadler
Indexer: Valerie Elliston
Production: Christina Schuster
Cover designed by Steve Woosnam-Savage

Originated in Singapore by Master Image
Printed and bound in Portugal by Printer Portuguesa

Contents

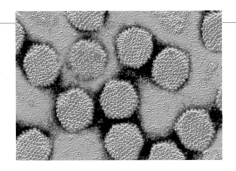

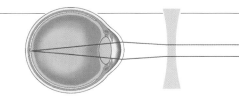

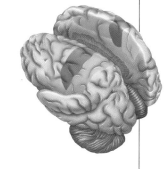

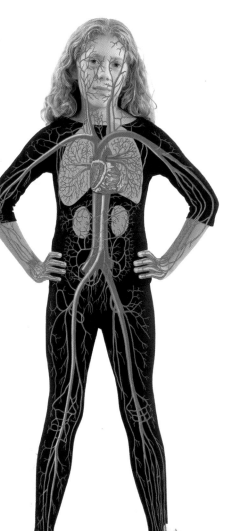

The Senses 52–53

The Cycle of Life 62–63

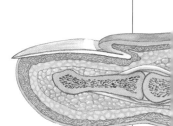

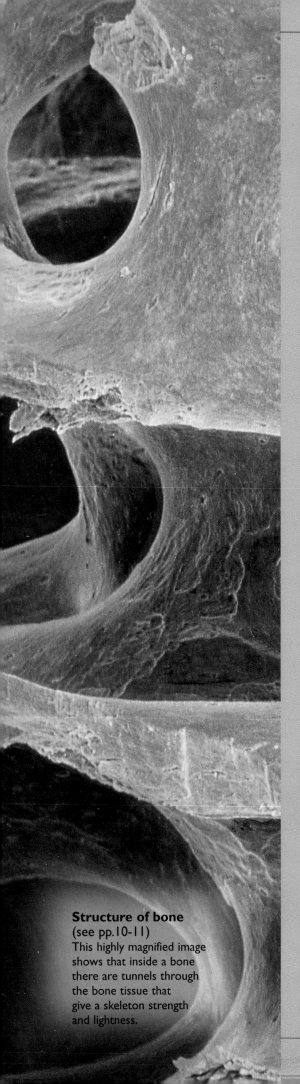

The Body's Framework

THE SHAPE OF YOUR BODY IS MADE by your bones, muscles and skin. Together they act like a kind of moving scaffold that is strong and flexible. Although we all have the same structure, our skin colour and body shape vary so that no two people are exactly alike.

Support and protection

Your skeleton supports the weight of your body and anything you carry. Powerful muscles pull on bones so that you can move and twist in many different directions. Covering the muscles is the body's biggest organ – the skin. Together, your skin, muscles and bones protect the soft organs packed inside your body.

Structure of bone (see pp.10-11)
This highly magnified image shows that inside a bone there are tunnels through the bone tissue that give a skeleton strength and lightness.

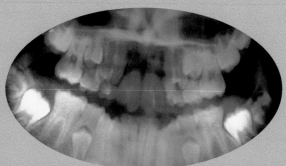

Teeth (see pp.10-11)
In this X-ray of a child's mouth, you can see that the two top front milk teeth have fallen out and been replaced by adult teeth. You can see the other adult teeth waiting to come through behind the milk teeth. Large molars are visible below the gums at the back and these will come through in early adulthood.

Skin (see pp.8-9)
This is a magnified view of the skin on the back of a hand. You can see tiny beads of sweat, too.

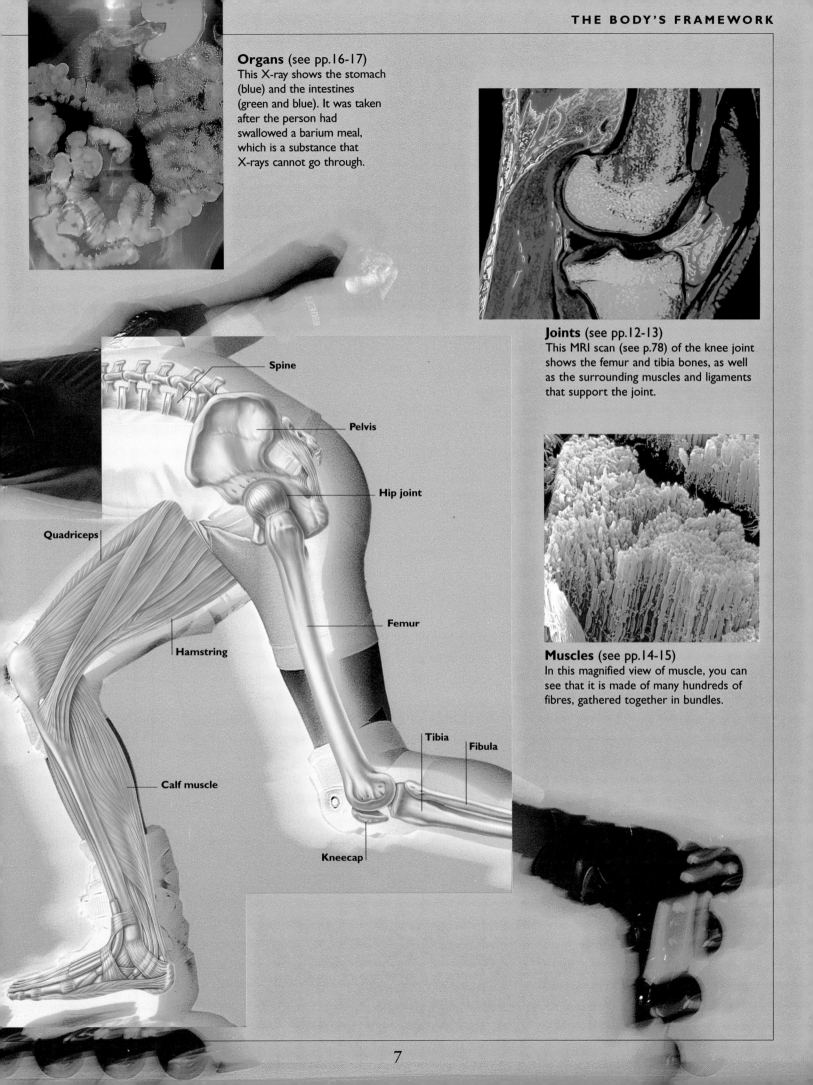

Organs (see pp.16-17)
This X-ray shows the stomach (blue) and the intestines (green and blue). It was taken after the person had swallowed a barium meal, which is a substance that X-rays cannot go through.

Joints (see pp.12-13)
This MRI scan (see p.78) of the knee joint shows the femur and tibia bones, as well as the surrounding muscles and ligaments that support the joint.

Muscles (see pp.14-15)
In this magnified view of muscle, you can see that it is made of many hundreds of fibres, gathered together in bundles.

Spine

Pelvis

Hip joint

Quadriceps

Femur

Hamstring

Tibia

Fibula

Calf muscle

Kneecap

Skin, Hair and Nails

Your skin, hair and nails do not just add to your appearance. They help to look after you. Through your skin you can feel warmth or cold, shape and texture, as well as pain. Your skin can also regulate your own body temperature and helps to make vitamin D, which you need to keep your bones healthy. You are covered from the top of your head to the soles of your feet in skin. In fact, your skin is the largest organ in your body. By the time you are a fully-grown adult, it will weigh around 5 kg (11 lb).

What is skin made from?

Your skin has two layers: the epidermis and the dermis. The epidermis is the outer layer, mostly made up of dead cells that constantly flake off. As they flake off, they are replaced by others that have made their way up from lower in the epidermis. The epidermis also produces sebum, the oil that makes your skin waterproof. Beneath the epidermis is a thicker layer known as the dermis. It contains blood vessels, nerves and sensors that detect touch, pressure, temperature and vibration (see p.54). Blood vessels in the dermis help with your temperature control (see right). Below the dermis is an insulating layer of subcutaneous fat.

Cross-section through the skin

Epidermis

Sweat pore

Sebaceous gland

Hair

Dermis

Fat

Hair follicle

Sebum

Sweat gland

Muscle

Artery

Dead cell layer

Living cell layer

Pressure sensor

Vein

Nerve

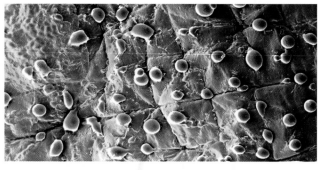

Skin changes

If you spend a long time in the bath, your skin's natural oil (sebum) is washed away. Your skin will start to absorb water and it will look wrinkled. Temperature also affects your skin's appearance. When you are cold, blood flow through the dermis is reduced to keep in body heat. This makes your skin look pale, and it feels cold. When you are warm, more blood flows through the dermis, so that you lose heat and your skin appears flushed and feels hot. If you get hot, your skin produces sweat through tiny pores (above), which helps to cool you down as it evaporates.

Why do you have hair?

Hair grows all over your body except on the palms of your hands and the soles of your feet. Each hair is made from dead cells. It has no feeling, but your skin can detect movement if something touches your hair, and in this way acts like a cat's whiskers. Hair is made of a substance called keratin, and can be dark or light, depending on the amount of melanin pigment in it (see below). There are around five million hairs altogether, about 100,000 of which are on your head. Your hair keeps you warm by reducing the heat lost through your head, like a hat. Your eyebrows and eyelashes protect your eyes by trapping dust and water.

Hair
Each hair grows for about a year before it falls out and is replaced by another one. If you never cut your hair, it would probably reach below your waist and then stop growing.

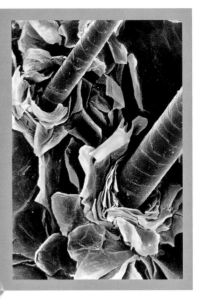

Fingernail
In this cross-section through a finger, you can see the nail matrix where new nail is formed. The nail lies on the nail bed which is packed with tiny blood vessels and nerves.

Lunula — Cuticle
Bone
Skin
Fat
Nail bed
Nail root
Nail matrix

Melanin
There are many different shades of skin colour. You have a pigment in your skin called melanin and the more you have, the darker your skin will be. Melanin helps protect your skin from the sun's harmful rays.

Why are nails useful?

Your nails are made mainly of keratin, like your hair, and protect the ends of your fingers. They also make it easier to grip and to pick up small objects – a small bead, for example, or to play an instrument, like a guitar. Your nail grows from just under the cuticle in the nail matrix, and in the white crescent-shaped area at the base of your nail known as the lunula.

Sweat

DID YOU KNOW?

Body debris
Most of the dust around you is made from skin cells. Every minute 30,000 dead skin cells fall off your body.

Thickest and thinnest
The skin on your eyelids is only about half a millimetre thick, compared to the skin on the sole of your foot, which is ten times thicker.

Hair versus nails
Everyone's hair grows at a different rate, but on average, your hair grows 5 mm a week while your fingernails grow by about 1 mm a week.

Bones and Teeth

Your skeleton and teeth make up one sixth of your body weight. The bones are made of millions of tiny building blocks called cells. These are supported by a framework of a substance called collagen, hardened with crystals of calcium and phosphorus. You have about 350 bones at birth but some fuse together, giving you just 206 bones by the time you're an adult. Teeth also have cells in the middle, surrounded by enamel. Your first teeth or 'milk teeth' are gradually replaced by a set of 32 permanent adult teeth.

What is a skeleton for?

For centuries, doctors and scientists have studied the bones and teeth of skeletons, but it was only after the invention of the X-ray, in 1895, that they could study them in living people. The skeleton provides a shape for the body and protects softer organs, such as the heart and brain, from being crushed. Muscles and ligaments attach to the bones so that the body can move. Women and girls tend to have lighter skeletons than men and boys, although a woman's pelvis is larger than a man's, to allow for a baby to pass through during birth.

Why do you need teeth?

Teeth give shape to your face and make it easier to talk, but their main function is to chew food. Adults usually have 16 teeth in each jaw: four incisors for cutting food, two canines for piercing, four premolars and six molars for grinding.

Changing teeth

Babies start to grow teeth at around six months. Most five-year-olds have a full set of 20 milk teeth, which later start to fall out to make room for the adult teeth. Most of your adult teeth will have appeared by the time you are 20.

Adult tooth waiting to emerge

Milk tooth

Adult front tooth

Emerging tooth

Molar

Incisor

Structure of a tooth

The soft pulp at the centre of a tooth contains blood vessels and nerves. Around it is a harder layer called dentine. Surrounding the dentine in the exposed part of the tooth is a very hard layer of enamel. Brushing your teeth regularly prevents plaque (a damaging mixture of mucus, food and germs) from attacking the enamel.

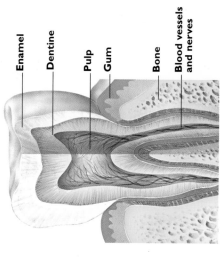

Enamel

Dentine

Pulp

Gum

Bone

Blood vessels and nerves

Skull

Orbit (eye socket)

Teeth

Clavicle (collar bone)

Scapula (shoulder blade)

Rib

Humerus

Sternum (breast bone)

Radius

Pelvis

Ulna

Vertebral column (spine)

KEEPING HEALTHY

Calcium

The body uses calcium to build strong bones and teeth. Calcium also helps your muscles to contract and relax properly. You need it for your nervous system, for defence against illness and for a healthy blood-clotting mechanism (see p.25). Your body gets calcium from food such as milk, cheese and some vegetables, such as watercress and broccoli. If you have too little calcium in your diet, you risk developing fragile bones in later life.

HELPING AND HEALING

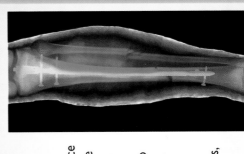

Pinned bones
This X-ray shows the pins holding together a broken tibia.

Broken bones

If you break a bone, it will mend itself because the bone cells divide to produce new bone at the site of the break. You need to keep it still in a cast or splint to allow the new soft bone to grow properly and harden. A bone that is broken in several places may be held together with metal screws, or pins.

Cross-section through the femur (thigh bone)

Spongy bone

Periosteum

Compact bone

Marrow

Blood vessels

Inside a bone

A long bone, such as the femur, has a cavity in the middle that is filled with marrow (see below). This is surrounded by light, spongy bone and around that is a shell of denser, heavier and stronger compact bone. The outer surface is covered by a membrane that contains nerves and blood vessels.

Bone marrow

While you are young, the marrow in your bones helps to produce new red and white blood cells. As you grow up, the marrow is gradually replaced by fat. By the time you're an adult, only a few bones, such as your ribs and sternum, still produce new blood cells.

Femur (thigh bone)

Tibia

Fibula

7 Tarsal bones (ankle bones)

8 Carpal bones (wrist bones)

DID YOU KNOW?

Hard stuff
The enamel on your teeth is the hardest substance in the whole of your body.

Biggest and smallest
The femur (thigh bone) is the biggest bone in the body. The smallest bone is the stapes, found in the inner ear.

Joints

A joint is formed where two bones meet. Most joints are moveable and are known as synovial joints. The range of movement in any synovial joint depends on its shape and on the way muscles and ligaments support it. You have several types of moveable joint to allow you different degrees of movement for various tasks. Ball and socket joints give you most movement, whereas the joints in your skull gradually become fixed after you are born.

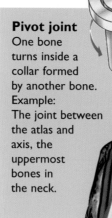

Pivot joint
One bone turns inside a collar formed by another bone. Example: The joint between the atlas and axis, the uppermost bones in the neck.

Atlas
Axis

Parietal bone
Suture
Frontal bone

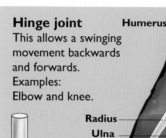

Hinge joint
This allows a swinging movement backwards and forwards.
Examples:
Elbow and knee.

Humerus

Radius
Ulna

Pelvis

Femur

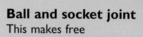

Ball and socket joint
This makes free movement possible in any direction.
Examples:
Shoulder and hip.

Why are there so many joints?

You need several different types of joints to move together so that you can carry out particular tasks, like kicking a ball, or writing a story. Some joints, such as those in your spine and pelvis, give less movement because the bones are needed for support. The joints in your skull become fixed to form a protective casing for your brain.

HELPING AND HEALING

Dislocated joints

Sudden force sometimes knocks a joint out of its normal position. This can happen when you injure yourself during a contact sport, such as football. It is most common in the ball and socket joints, such as the shoulder. It is painful because the bones are not in their normal position and movement is restricted. Doctors can gently pull the bones and click them back in place.

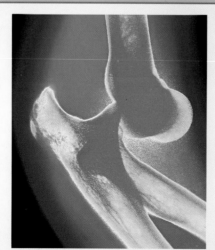

Dislocation

This is an X-ray of a dislocated elbow joint showing the bones knocked out of their normal position.

Fixed joint
A few joints in the body are fixed, allowing little or no movement. The two bones are bound together with fibrous tissue. Fixed joints in the skull are known as sutures because they 'stitch' the skull together.

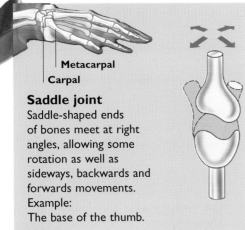

Metacarpal
Carpal

Saddle joint
Saddle-shaped ends of bones meet at right angles, allowing some rotation as well as sideways, backwards and forwards movements.
Example:
The base of the thumb.

What is inside a joint?
Apart from the bones, moveable joints are made up of cartilage, fluid and ligaments. Some joints also contain fat, to act as a shock absorber. Cartilage forms a smooth surface so bones can move easily over each other. The fluid lubricates the joint. Ligaments are thickened parts of the joint capsule that prevent too much movement. In a fetus, almost all the bones are made of cartilage (see pp.72-73).

Knee joint
In this MRI scan (see p.78) of the knee joint, you can see the white cartilage at the end of the bones.

Cross-section through a knee joint

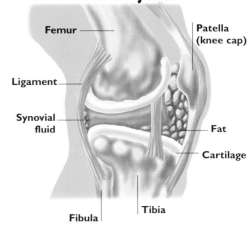

Femur
Patella (knee cap)
Ligament
Synovial fluid
Fat
Cartilage
Fibula
Tibia

Holding it together
Ligaments prevent a joint from moving too much. Some ligaments stretch right across the joint attaching to bone on either side.

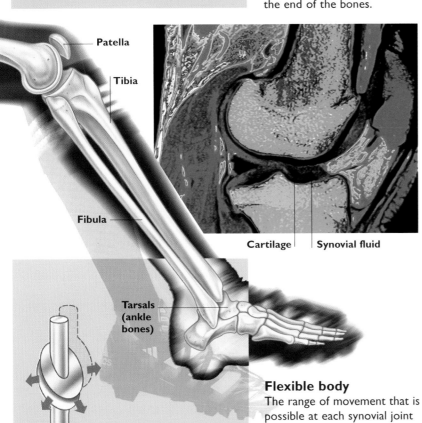

Patella
Tibia
Fibula
Tarsals (ankle bones)

Cartilage | Synovial fluid

Gliding joint
The bones have flat surfaces that allow limited movement only.
Examples:
Carpal bones of the wrist and tarsal bones of the ankle.

Flexible body
The range of movement that is possible at each synovial joint varies between individuals. The body needs to be flexible enough to carry out normal daily tasks. People such as gymnasts are unusually flexible.

KEEPING HEALTHY

Staying flexible
A mobile spine and flexible joints prevent muscle strain and backache and improve overall athletic performance. Girls tend to be more flexible than boys, but once they reach adolescence their flexibility declines and there is less difference in adults. The commonest reason for a loss of flexibility is lack of exercise.

Stretch out
Flexibility is improved by warming up and stretching exercises.

DID YOU KNOW?

Double joints
Some people are very flexible, but although they are sometimes described as 'double jointed' they have the same number of joints as the rest of us.

Clicking joints
Ever wondered what causes the noise you make when your joints click? The sound is made as the synovial fluid moves from one place to another inside the joint.

Muscles

The human body contains many hundreds of muscles. When any muscle shortens, or contracts, it produces a movement. A small movement, such as a blink, only uses a few muscles, while an action like walking needs many groups of muscles working together. Babies have to learn to control their muscles so they can walk and feed themselves. But some muscles, such as heart muscle, can't be controlled this way.

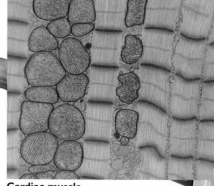
Cardiac muscle

Where are your muscles?

There are three types of muscle in your body. Cardiac muscle is found only in the heart. It contracts regularly, without getting tired, and your life depends upon it. Smooth muscle is found in the walls of your intestines, your blood vessels, your bladder and many other organs in your body. Most smooth muscle contracts without you knowing it, for example to push food along the intestines. Skeletal muscle is the type that most of us refer to when we are exercising. It is the type that covers and moves the bones of the skeleton.

Cardiac muscle
In this magnified image of heart muscle, the pink areas are muscle fibres. The dark oval shapes are structures that produce energy for the muscle.

Smooth muscle

Smooth muscle
This image shows red muscle fibres in the walls of a fallopian tube (see p.70).

Skeletal muscle
Much of this image is taken up by a single muscle fibre. The vertical strands in the fibre are individual fibrils.

What are most muscles made from?

Your skeletal muscle is formed from bundles of closely-packed muscle fibres. Each muscle fibre is a cell made of fibrils. Within each fibril are strands of thick and thin filaments. When a message is sent along a nerve to the muscle, it makes the filaments slide between each other. As a result, each fibril shortens. When all the fibrils shorten together, the whole muscle shortens, or contracts.

Skeletal muscle

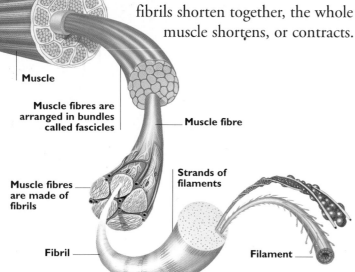

Muscle

Muscle fibres are arranged in bundles called fascicles

Muscle fibre

Muscle fibres are made of fibrils

Strands of filaments

Fibril

Filament

KEEPING HEALTHY

Protecting your muscles
To prevent injury when you exercise, or play sport, it's very important that you warm up and stretch your muscles first. Start by walking or jogging slowly for five minutes until you feel warm. Follow a recommended series of stretches. Hold each of your stretches for at least ten seconds. Try to avoid bouncing or jerking against the muscle.

Some muscles in the body

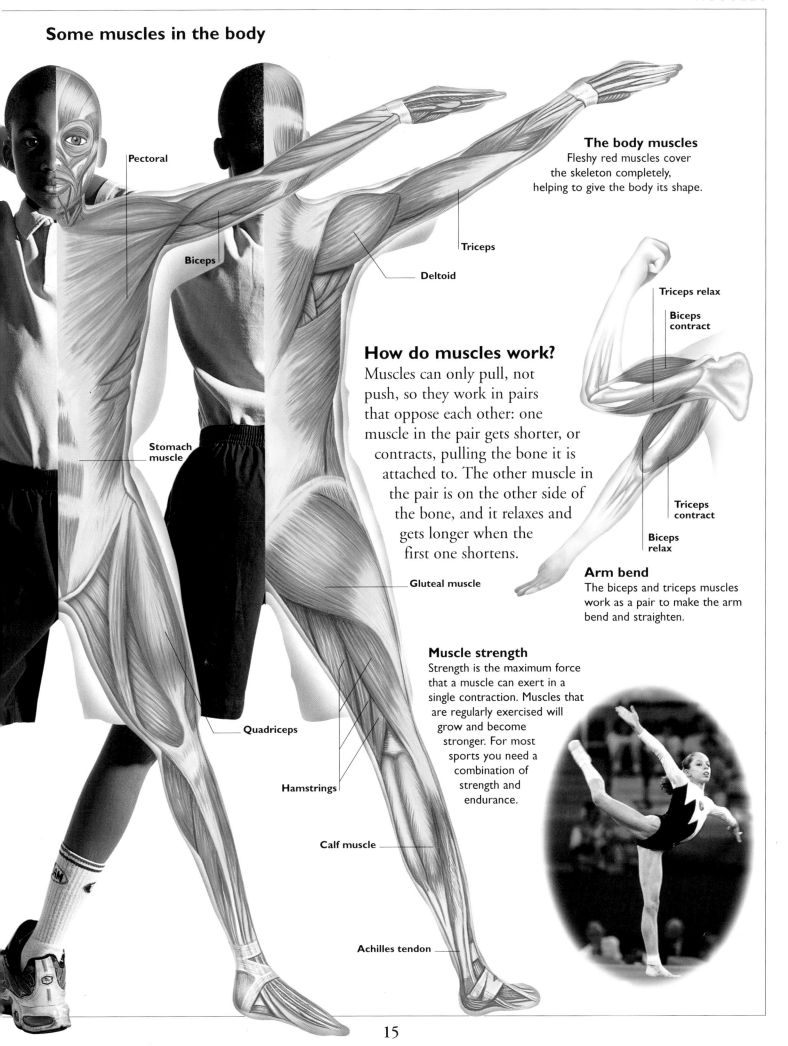

Pectoral

Biceps

Triceps

Deltoid

Stomach muscle

Gluteal muscle

Quadriceps

Hamstrings

Calf muscle

Achilles tendon

The body muscles
Fleshy red muscles cover the skeleton completely, helping to give the body its shape.

How do muscles work?
Muscles can only pull, not push, so they work in pairs that oppose each other: one muscle in the pair gets shorter, or contracts, pulling the bone it is attached to. The other muscle in the pair is on the other side of the bone, and it relaxes and gets longer when the first one shortens.

Triceps relax

Biceps contract

Triceps contract

Biceps relax

Arm bend
The biceps and triceps muscles work as a pair to make the arm bend and straighten.

Muscle strength
Strength is the maximum force that a muscle can exert in a single contraction. Muscles that are regularly exercised will grow and become stronger. For most sports you need a combination of strength and endurance.

Body Organs

Each organ packed inside your body does a particular job. Some organs work together – for example, the stomach, liver, gallbladder, pancreas and intestines cooperate to extract and process nutrients from food. Together, these organs form the digestive system. Whatever its function, every organ is part of a complete working machine, so if disease threatens any one of them, your whole body could be affected.

What organs are in your torso?

One large organ, the skin, covers your body (see p.8). Apart from the organs in your head, most others are packed tightly inside your torso. These include your heart, your lungs, the organs of your digestive system, your kidneys and your bladder. The torso also contains the spleen (an organ that removes worn-out blood cells and helps fight infection), the adrenal glands (which make a number of important hormones), many large blood vessels, and, in girls, the uterus or womb.

Lungs
Air enters your lungs via a branching network of tubes, shown here in an X-ray of one lung.

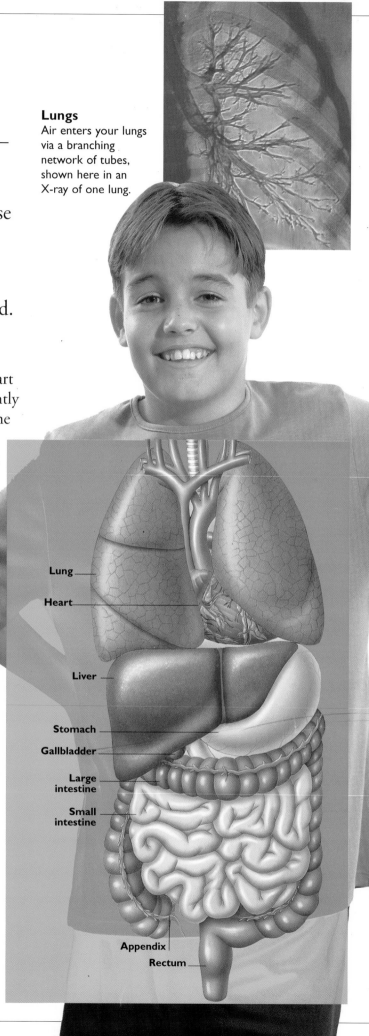

Lung

Heart

Liver

Stomach

Gallbladder

Large intestine

Small intestine

Appendix

Rectum

Stomach and intestines
The stomach (blue area at the top of this X-ray) and intestines (green) break down the food you eat and extract nutrients and water from it.

DID YOU KNOW?

Mirror image
In extremely rare cases, a person's organs are in opposite positions in the body from where they are expected. This can happen in identical twins where one twin is the mirror image of the other. The medical term for this is situs inversus.

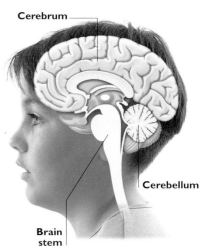

What organs are in your head?

Most of the organs you need to interact with the world around you are inside your head. Your skull contains your brain, the body's control centre, which has three main parts: the brain stem, cerebellum, and cerebrum (see p.43). Also protected by the skull are the sense organs – the eyes, nose, ears, and taste buds in your mouth – which help to gather information about your surroundings. Because the head has such an important role in your body, it has a large blood supply, delivering essential nutrients and oxygen to the brain and sense organs.

Cerebrum

Cerebellum

Brain stem

Heart
The heart (purple area in this X-ray) is a hollow muscle that pumps blood to all the other organs in the body (see p.22).

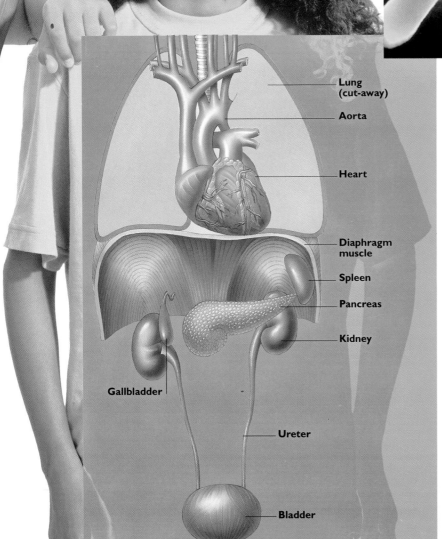

Lung (cut-away)

Aorta

Heart

Diaphragm muscle

Spleen

Pancreas

Kidney

Gallbladder

Ureter

Bladder

Liver and gallbladder
The liver (yellow-green area in this X-ray) is the largest internal organ. One of its many functions is to make bile, which helps to digest fats (see p.34). It also stores energy and breaks down alcohol. The gallbladder (yellow-brown sac at left of the X-ray) temporarily stores bile before releasing it into the small intestine.

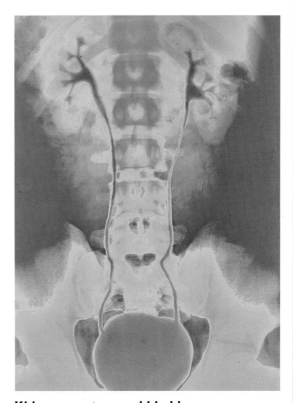

Kidneys, ureters and bladder
The kidneys (green areas at top of X-ray) remove wastes from the blood and dispose of them in urine (see pp.36–37). The urine flows via ducts called ureters to the bladder (red area at bottom). This stores the urine until you can pass it from the body.

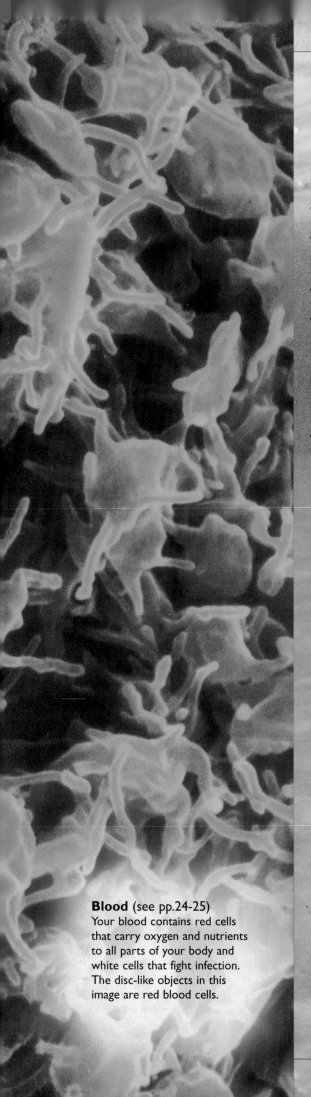

Body Maintenance

FOR YOUR BODY TO WORK NORMALLY,
all parts of it require a supply of nutrients
and oxygen. The oxygen is supplied by
breathing, and nutrients come from the food
you eat. Both oxygen and nutrients pass into
your bloodstream and are pumped by the
heart to areas that need them. Your body
has defence mechanisms to fight against
infection, and wastes are disposed of via
your kidneys, intestines and lungs.

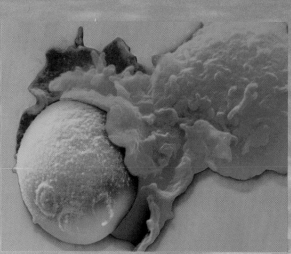

Blood (see pp.24-25)
Your blood contains red cells
that carry oxygen and nutrients
to all parts of your body and
white cells that fight infection.
The disc-like objects in this
image are red blood cells.

Fighting infection (see pp.28-29)
Your body is under attack constantly from germs.
Most germs are defeated by the body's defence
system, which includes white blood cells.
The white cell shown above is digesting
a yeast cell, which is one type of
germ. Lymph vessels and lymph
glands are also part of the
defence system.

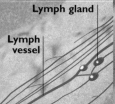

Lymph gland

Lymph
vessel

Heart and circulation
(see pp.20-23)
Your heart is a muscular organ that pumps blood around your body via a network of blood vessels. This image of the heart was made by a method called angiography (see p.78).

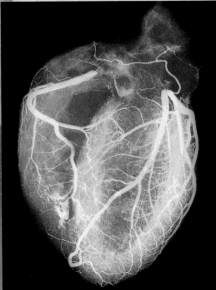

Hormones (see pp.38-39)
One of the body's main hormones is insulin, which some pople have to self-inject.

Maintaining a steady state
During the day your body experiences many changes. Some of the time you are eating, sometimes exercising or resting, sometimes exposed to cold and sometimes in the warm. Despite these changes in your environment and routine, inside your body everything remains fairly constant. Special chemicals released within the body called hormones play a part in maintaining this steady state. Hormones also control your growth.

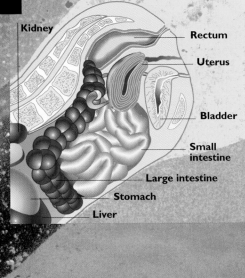

Kidney
Rectum
Uterus
Bladder
Small intestine
Large intestine
Stomach
Liver

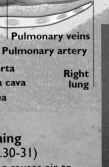

Heart

Pulmonary veins
Pulmonary artery
Aorta
Vena cava
Trachea
Right lung

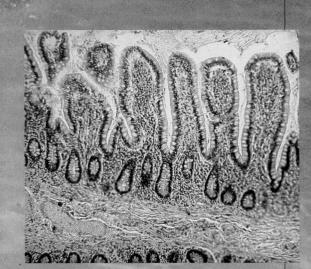

Digesting and processing waste
(see pp.34-37)
Food and drink provide you with energy and other nutrients that you need to make your organs work normally. Nutrients pass through the wall of your intestine (of which a microscopic view is shown above) and into the bloodstream. Your body also produces wastes, which are disposed of when you go to the toilet.

Breathing
(see pp.30-31)
Breathing causes air to flow into and out of your lungs. Your lungs are made of millions of tiny air pockets that are like leaves at the end of branches, as shown here.

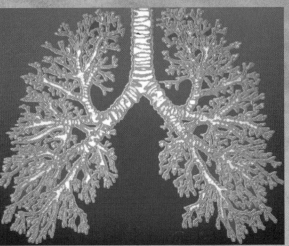

Circulation

To survive, your body needs a constant supply of oxygen, energy and nutrients produced from food. You also need to get rid of waste products such as carbon dioxide and urea. These supplies and wastes are all transported in your blood inside a network of blood vessels that reaches every part of your body. To move the blood around, you have a muscular pump inside your chest known as your heart. This constant movement of blood is known as your circulation.

Your blood vessels
Blood circulates around your body in arteries (red) and veins (blue). This network reaches into every part of your body.

Carotid artery

Heart

Aorta

Femoral artery

Femoral vein

What are veins and arteries?

Blood that contains oxygen is pumped from your heart in blood vessels called arteries. Blood containing wastes is carried back to the heart by blood vessels known as veins. Arteries and veins branch and divide the farther they are from your heart, so that they can reach every muscle, bone and organ in your body. You have so many blood vessels that if they were all laid end to end they would stretch around the world twice!

Little artery
In the centre of this magnified view of a small artery, you can see some red blood cells.

TRY IT YOURSELF

Feeling drained?

Blood is constantly circulating through the small arteries, capillaries and small veins in your fingers. You can see the effects of this very easily:

• Press firmly with a finger on the soft end part of your thumb.

• Take your finger away – the skin on your thumb will be pale. This is because you emptied the capillaries when you pressed on your thumb tip.

• It quickly becomes pink again as the capillaries are filled from the small arteries.

DID YOU KNOW?

Liquid asset
An average adult body has about 5 litres of blood in the circulation. At any one time, around one litre is in the arteries, around 250 ml is in the capillaries and the rest is in the veins.

Deep down
Most of your arteries are positioned deeper in your skin than your veins. Most cuts bleed from small veins near to the surface.

How does circulation work?

It is common to refer to your heart as a pump, but it is really two pumps working together. One side of your heart pumps blood from your body to your lungs, where it absorbs oxygen then returns to the heart. The other side pumps blood coming back from the lungs to the rest of your body, so the organs can get the oxygen they need. Arteries carrying blood from the heart divide into smaller vessels called arterioles and then into capillaries, from which oxygen and other nutrients are absorbed by the tissues of your body. In return, waste products from your tissues are delivered to the capillaries, which join up to form venules and then veins, which carry blood back to the heart.

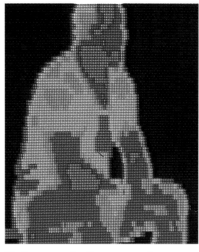

Before and after exercise
During exercise, more blood goes to your muscles and skin, from where heat can escape to help stop you overheating. The thermograms (heat images) above show a person before (left) and after exercise. The red and yellow areas in the second image show the regions giving off most heat.

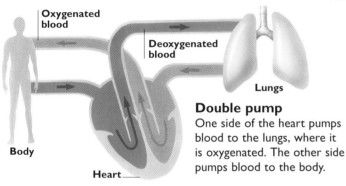

Double pump
One side of the heart pumps blood to the lungs, where it is oxygenated. The other side pumps blood to the body.

Nutrient exchange in the blood

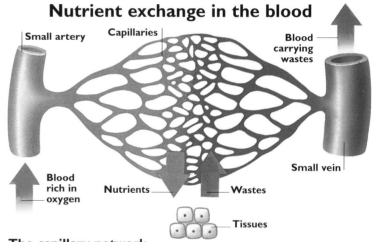

The capillary network
Capillary walls have spaces through which nutrients flow out into body tissues and waste products come in.

Why is blood pressure important?

When your heart pumps blood to the body, it produces a wave of pressure that pushes the blood to your organs and tissues. High blood pressure can cause damage to your organs and blood vessels. If the pressure is too low, organs may not get enough oxygen and may not be able to work properly. This pressure wave can be measured in the main artery in your arm using a machine called a sphygmomanometer.

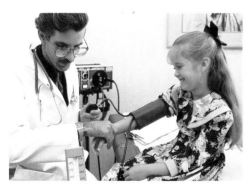

Measuring blood pressure
Blood pressure is measured using a cuff on your arm and a stethoscope on your artery.

KEEPING HEALTHY

Taking exercise

Regular exercise helps to strengthen your heart and keep your blood pressure at healthy levels. You may already take part in sports such as football or swimming, but exercise can also be a part of your daily routine. Try walking to school instead of taking the bus, for example. When you are exercising, your muscles need more blood, so it is diverted from other parts of your body, such as your digestive system. If you exercise too soon after eating, not enough blood can be channelled to your muscles, and you may feel cramp in your legs or a stitch in your side.

Pedal power
Riding a bike is excellent exercise – try doing it every day to keep fit.

The Heart

Your heart is a hollow muscle, about the size of your fist, sandwiched between your lungs and protected by your rib cage. It beats about 60 times a minute, and each beat pushes blood around your body. Your heart has four chambers: two atria and two ventricles. The coronary arteries give the heart a constant supply of oxygen and nutrients. If your heart stopped working, you would die within a few minutes.

What is inside your heart?

Your heart is like two pumps working side by side (see p.21). Each pump has two compartments: a small atrium, with thin walls, and a larger ventricle with more muscular walls. The right atrium and ventricle are separated from the left atrium and ventricle by a thick muscle called the septum. In the model below, you can see that the right side of the heart lies a little below the left side. The blood vessels entering and leaving the heart twist around each other.

Blood supply to your heart

Your heart needs oxygen and energy just like all the other parts of your body. It has its own supply of blood, known as the coronary circulation. It is these arteries, visible in this X-ray, that can become diseased and blocked so that not enough oxygen gets to the heart muscle. The muscle may die and this is called a 'heart attack', or 'coronary'.

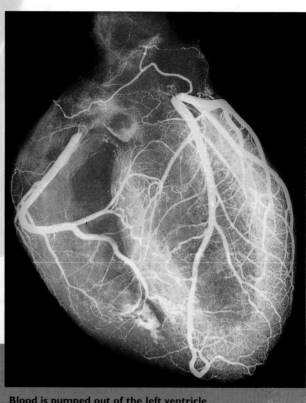

Blood flow in the heart

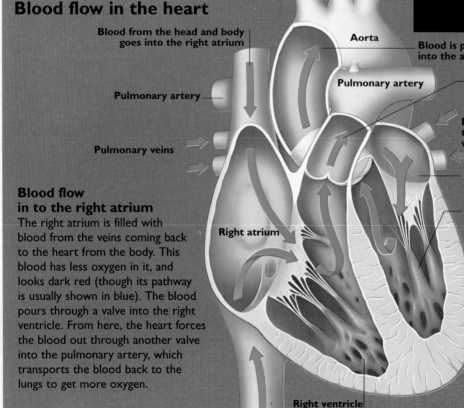

Blood from the head and body goes into the right atrium

Aorta

Blood is pumped out of the left ventricle into the aorta to the head and body

Pulmonary artery

Blood leaves the right ventricle in the pulmonary artery and goes to the lungs

Pulmonary artery

Blood from the lungs goes through the pulmonary veins into the left atrium

Pulmonary veins

Left atrium

Left ventricle

Right atrium

Right ventricle

Blood flow in to the right atrium

The right atrium is filled with blood from the veins coming back to the heart from the body. This blood has less oxygen in it, and looks dark red (though its pathway is usually shown in blue). The blood pours through a valve into the right ventricle. From here, the heart forces the blood out through another valve into the pulmonary artery, which transports the blood back to the lungs to get more oxygen.

Blood flow in to the left atrium

The blood that fills the left atrium has come from your lungs and is full of oxygen, which makes it appear bright red. It drains into the left ventricle through a valve. The left ventricle pumps this blood out of the heart and into the aorta through a valve. From the aorta, the blood flows to the brain and the rest of the body.

What is a heartbeat?

A heart beat is the whole sequence of actions in which your heart first fills with blood and then empties again. If you are resting, or reading quietly, your heart muscle beats about 60-80 times a minute. If you go for a ride on your bike, your heart beat may increase up to 200 beats a minute. Your heart beat may also rise if you are stressed, such as when you are watching a frightening film, or before a performance (see p.49). At times like these you may be able to feel your heart beating fast, thumping in your chest, even though you are not exercising.

What are heart sounds?

If you put your ear close to a friend's chest, you may be able to hear the sounds of his or her heart beating. A doctor can hear the same sounds using an instrument called a stethoscope. The sounds are made as the heart valves open and close. If blood is not flowing normally, the doctor may hear a sound called a 'murmur'. Not all heart murmurs are abnormal.

Monitoring your heartbeat

In this painless test, electrodes are attached to your chest, arms and legs, to detect the electrical activity in your heart. The pattern it makes is known as your electrocardiogram, or ECG. A healthy heart has a characteristic ECG pattern of peaks and troughs.

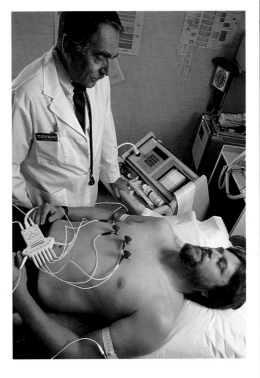

What are heart valves?

The atria and ventricles are separated by valves, which are like one-way doors, helping to make sure that blood flows in the right direction through the heart. The aorta and the pulmonary artery also have large valves to prevent blood that has been pumped out of the ventricles from flowing back into the heart again.

Atria fill
Blood from body
Blood from the lungs
Blood from body

Ventricles fill
Valve opens
Valve opens
Valve closes

Ventricles empty
Blood to the body
Blood to the lungs
Valve closes
Valve closes

A heartbeat

The heart muscle relaxes and blood flows in, via the atria, to fill the ventricles. Then the ventricles squeeze blood out of the heart, forcing shut the valves between the atria and ventricles. As the heart relaxes, the valves in the aorta and pulmonary artery snap shut.

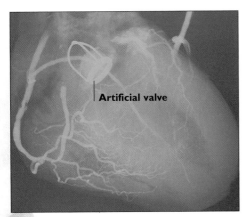

Artificial valve

Replacement valves

Occasionally a heart valve becomes damaged and needs to be replaced with a new one. Replacement valves can come from pigs, or from donated human hearts, or they can be made artificially (above). During an operation to replace a valve, the heart is stopped, so that the surgeon can operate. When the new valve is in place, the heart is re-started.

KEEPING HEALTHY

Healthy heart watch

• Like all the other muscles in your body, your heart muscle needs exercise to keep it fit. To be of any benefit, you have to exercise regularly and continue exercising as you get older.

• Your diet also influences the fitness of your heart. Diets that limit the amount of animal fat you eat are ideal. Animal fat is found in red meat and dairy products such as butter, cream and cheese.

• Smoking and alcohol can damage your heart muscle.

Blood

One of your earliest discoveries in life is that when you fall and cut yourself, you lose some blood – the sticky red fluid that circulates around your body in blood vessels. In fact, every drop of blood travels round your body about a thousand times a day. Each drop is delivering oxygen, energy and nutrients to wherever they are needed. On the same journey, your blood is collecting waste products for disposal (see p.36). New blood cells are made all the time in the marrow of long bones and once you are an adult you will have about five litres of blood in your body.

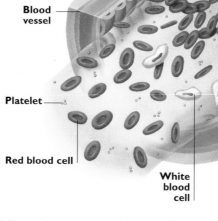

Blood vessel

Platelet

Red blood cell

White blood cell

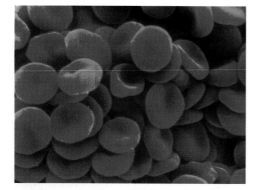

Red blood cells
These are produced in your bone marrow and carry oxygen to all your tissues around the body. They live for about three months and then get broken up in your spleen.

What is in your blood?
Just under half your blood consists of cells. The rest is made up of plasma. Plasma is mostly water and gives blood its fluidity. Red cells transport oxygen to the body, white cells fight infection and the platelets help blood to clot or form a scab (see opposite). Blood also carries essential nutrients such as glucose and calcium that have been absorbed from your digestive system, and it transports the hormones produced by your body (see p.38). Blood helps clean away waste products like carbon dioxide and urea, taking them to the lungs (see p.30) or kidneys (see p.36) for disposal.

The constituents of blood
If you allow your blood to settle in a test tube, it separates out into its various constituents. The red blood cells are the heaviest constituent and they sink to the bottom of the tube.

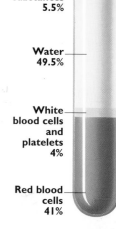

Dissolved substances 5.5%

Water 49.5%

White blood cells and platelets 4%

Red blood cells 41%

White blood cell
This is a type of white cell called a lymphocyte. It plays an important part in the immune response of your body.

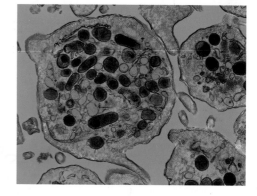

Platelets
These tiny cells clump together to form a plug and prevent blood leaking from damaged blood vessels.

Why is your blood red?

Red blood cells contain a pigment called haemoglobin, which is made partly of iron. This pigment gives the blood its characteristic colour. When blood passes through the lungs, the haemoglobin attracts oxygen and binds to it. The oxygen is carried around your body, attached to haemoglobin, until it reaches a part that needs it. Then the oxygen separates from the haemoglobin.

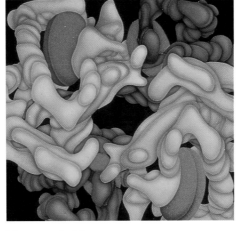

Haemoglobin
This is a computer generated picture of the structure of haemoglobin.

Clotting

Soon after a blood vessel is damaged, platelets clump together to make a kind of plug (A). With the help of a substance called fibrin, they gradually form a mesh. Red blood cells are trapped in the mesh, becoming a blood clot. A blood clot on the surface of your body is better known as a scab (B). If you injure yourself without breaking the surface of your skin, the blood may leak into your skin from damaged blood vessels, forming a purple or red mark known as a bruise.

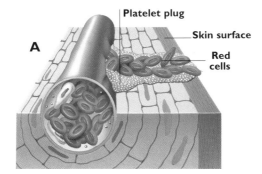

A — Platelet plug, Skin surface, Red cells

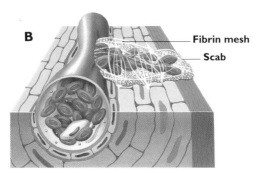

B — Fibrin mesh, Scab

Bruising

If small blood vessels are damaged but the skin is not broken, a bruise will form (right).

What is your blood group?

On the surface of every red blood cell is a small structure that determines which blood group you belong to. There are four main groups: A, B, AB, and O.

Your body cannot survive without a certain quantity of blood in circulation. If you have an accident or a major surgical operation, you may need to replace lost blood through a transfusion. This is when you are given blood previously collected from another person and stored in a blood bank. You receive the blood through a small tube connected to one of your veins. Before you are given blood, a number of tests are carried out to discover your blood group. This ensures that you receive blood that is well matched with yours. This prevents the new supply from reacting with your own blood.

Natural Barriers

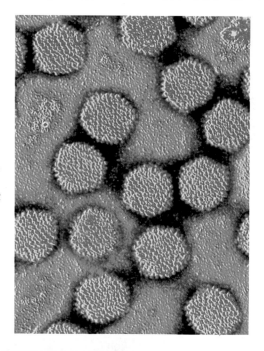

If you look around your bedroom you may be able to see places that need cleaning, but you will not be able to see the millions of germs living in the dust and covering your skin and clothes. Germs also live in your intestines, on your food, in your water and in the soil. They are invisible to the naked eye, but if a germ multiplies inside your body, it becomes an infection. However, although you are surrounded by germs, your body's defences usually help to prevent an infection. These natural barriers form part of your immune system.

What are germs?

Germs include bacteria and viruses. Bacteria are living organisms made of single cells. Most are harmless, but some, such as meningitis bacteria, can cause very serious infections. Viruses are smaller than bacteria and can only survive by taking over other cells. Viruses are responsible for most of the common infections, such as coughs and colds, and some more serious ones such as HIV infection.

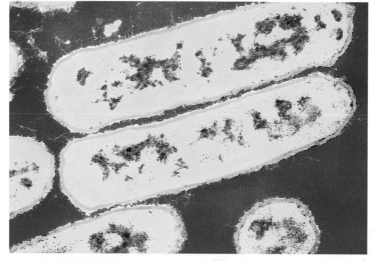

Virus
The dozen or so orange objects seen above are individual particles of a virus. This virus causes breathing problems, colds, and children's diarrhoea.

Bacteria
These bacteria (left) cause bronchitis, pneumonia and bacterial meningitis.

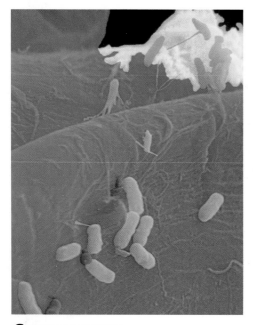

Germs on a mug
Thorough cleaning with a simple detergent will remove most but not all germs.

Sneezing
When you sneeze (left), thousands of droplets of saliva and mucus shoot out of your nose and mouth at over 64 km per hour. They may be spread as far as 10 meters away.

How do you spread germs?

Germs trapped by natural barriers such as the mucus in your nose can be expelled from your body by coughing or sneezing. But germs can also be spread this way, which is why you should cover your mouth and nose when you cough or sneeze. This action helps to prevent the germs from landing on other people and infecting them.

How does your body protect you from germs?

Although germs cover your skin and intestine, they usually cause no harm. It is only when one of the germs manages to get through the skin or into the organs that it can multiply and cause problems. So it is important that your body stops germs from getting inside. It has many very effective defences, which are shown here.

Tears
Tears wash away germs. Tears also contain chemicals that attack germs.

Mucus
Germs in the air that you breathe in are trapped in the thick mucus in your nose. Sneezing or blowing your nose gets rid of them.

The skin
Just as tiles on a roof prevent water from getting in, the outer layer of your skin is made of dead cells that provide a barrier to germs. Your skin also contains sebaceous glands (see p.8) that produce an oil to poison germs.

Sweat
Your skin produces sweat that flushes away germs.

Stomach acid
The acid produced in your stomach to digest food also destroys most germs that you have eaten.

Urine
The flow of urine washes germs away from your body,

KEEPING HEALTHY

Washing
You can help to avoid infections by always washing your hands before eating. Drying your hands is also important as germs prefer moist places. Because germs live in the soil, it is important to make sure that salads and vegetables are cleaned thoroughly before you eat them. Many germs are killed by high temperatures so any germs not washed away are usually destroyed by cooking. Always make sure that the cooked food you eat is piping hot all the way through.

Debugging
A good wash with soap and water rids your skin of most germs.

DID YOU KNOW?

Good germs?
Germs can be useful: about half of your daily requirement of vitamin K is produced by some of the germs that live in your intestine.

Germ clusters
There are about 100 million germs in every 1 ml of saliva. The plaque on your teeth is made up almost entirely of germs.

Exterminate
You can get rid of most germs from food or textiles by boiling them in water for more than a minute.

Close to the skin
Clumps of bacteria live on your skin, from 100 to 10,000 of them in every square centimetre.

Fighting Infection

If a germ penetrates the body's natural barriers (see p.26) and multiplies, it causes an infection. Infections can be minor, like a boil, or they can be more serious, like pneumonia. To fight infections, your body has a mini army of special cells and organs that work together to make up your immune system. When this system is stimulated, it produces an immune reaction. This reaction alters your immune system permanently, so that the next time it is exposed to the same germ, your body can react more quickly to destroy the infection.

How does a germ invade?

Most of us have fallen over and cut ourselves at some time. Usually the broken skin heals up without any problem. But occasionally, the wound can become infected. This is because the germs that usually live on the surface of your skin have broken through the body's natural barriers and started to multiply inside the body. You can tell that a small cut is becoming infected because it feels hot and looks swollen and redder than usual. This appearance is also called 'inflammation', and it feels very sore.

What happens once the germ invades?

Germs causing the inflammation are attacked and engulfed by white blood cells called macrophages. Any germs that have made their way to the bloodstream circulate around the body. The blood is filtered through large quantities of macrophages situated in the liver, kidney and spleen.

Your normal body temperature is between 35.8 and 37.5°C. If you've a cold or any other infection, the macrophages produce a chemical that resets your body's thermostat, so your temperature rises.

How does a germ invade?

I. If the skin's surface is broken, the damaged cells release chemicals such as histamine. This makes nearby blood vessels leaky and brings white blood cells, known as macrophages, into the damaged area.

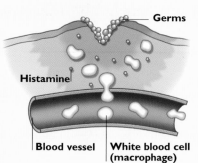

Germs

Histamine

Blood vessel

White blood cell (macrophage)

2. The macrophages engulf the germs and are absorbed in the lymphatic system.

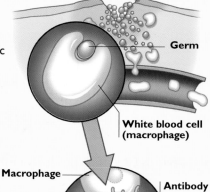

Germ

White blood cell (macrophage)

3. In the lymph node, a macrophage shows the germ to white cells called B lymphocytes. These produce antibodies to the germ.

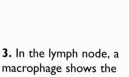

Macrophage

Antibody

B lymphocyte in lymph node

4. Antibodies are sent in the blood to the infected area, where they attach to the germs. The germs and antibodies are then engulfed and destroyed by phagocytes.

Antibody attaches to germ

Phagocyte

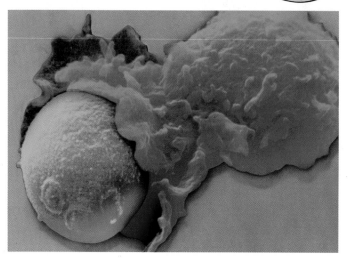

Phagocyte

A phagocyte is a type of white blood cell that engulfs and digests germs. In the highly magnified photograph on the left, the blue shape is the phagocyte, shown surrounding the yellow yeast cell before destroying it.

What is the lymphatic system?

Once they have been attacked by the macrophages, the germs are carried in small channels, known as lymphatics, to the lymph nodes and spleen. Here the germs are met by white cells called lymphocytes. There are two kinds of lymphocytes: B lymphocytes, which make antibodies to attack and destroy germs, while T lymphocytes help B cells produce antibodies, and control the activities of other cells such as macrophages.

Lymph channel

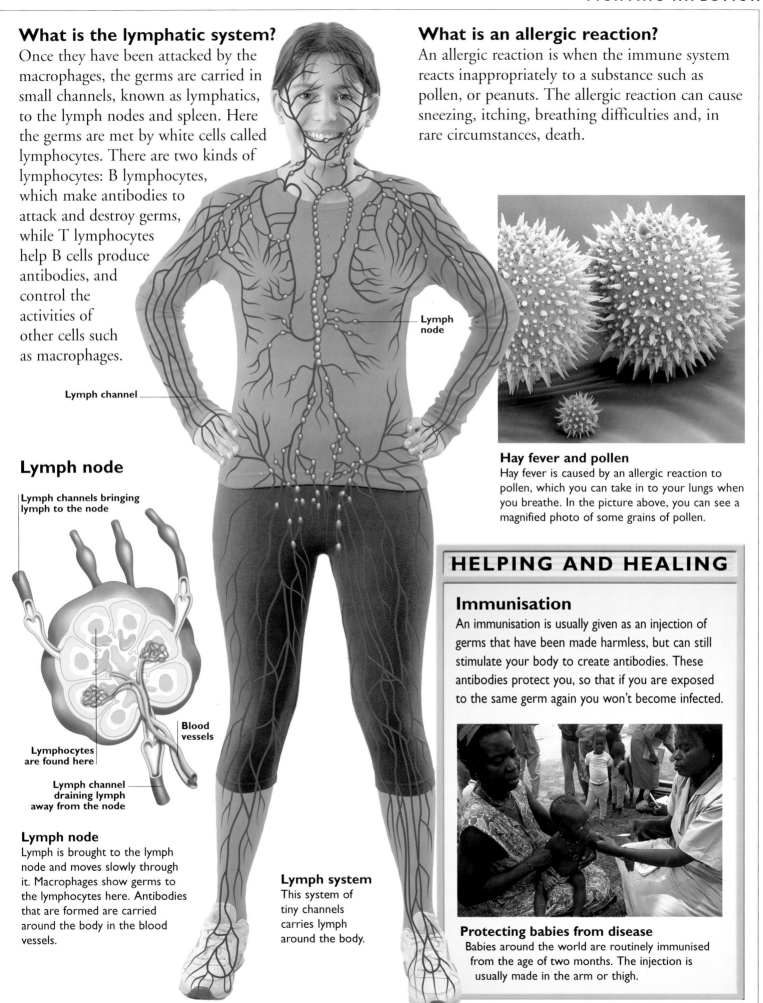

Lymph node

Lymph node

Lymph channels bringing lymph to the node

Lymphocytes are found here

Blood vessels

Lymph channel draining lymph away from the node

Lymph node

Lymph is brought to the lymph node and moves slowly through it. Macrophages show germs to the lymphocytes here. Antibodies that are formed are carried around the body in the blood vessels.

Lymph system

This system of tiny channels carries lymph around the body.

What is an allergic reaction?

An allergic reaction is when the immune system reacts inappropriately to a substance such as pollen, or peanuts. The allergic reaction can cause sneezing, itching, breathing difficulties and, in rare circumstances, death.

Hay fever and pollen

Hay fever is caused by an allergic reaction to pollen, which you can take in to your lungs when you breathe. In the picture above, you can see a magnified photo of some grains of pollen.

HELPING AND HEALING

Immunisation

An immunisation is usually given as an injection of germs that have been made harmless, but can still stimulate your body to create antibodies. These antibodies protect you, so that if you are exposed to the same germ again you won't become infected.

Protecting babies from disease

Babies around the world are routinely immunised from the age of two months. The injection is usually made in the arm or thigh.

Breathing

Without a supply of air, none of us could survive. With each breath, you suck air into your lungs to extract oxygen from it. The oxygen is absorbed into your blood where it is carried in your red blood cells to the rest of your body (see p.24). Body cells produce carbon dioxide as a waste product gas, that is dissolved in the blood and breathed out from your lungs. You are unaware of your breathing unless you are not getting enough oxygen – when you are underwater, or exercising hard, for example. Your brain is in overall charge of breathing, but you can decide when to breathe more quickly, or more slowly.

What happens when you breathe?

When you breathe in, air is warmed and filtered by little hairs and mucus in your nose which remove any dust particles. You have two lungs inside your chest, protected by ribs and muscle. Air passes into your trachea, more often known as your windpipe, past your vocal cords and into a branching system of tubes, called bronchi, which get smaller and smaller until they end in millions of tiny pouches known as alveoli, or air sacs (see below). The walls of the alveoli are thin, and in close contact with small blood vessels, known as capillaries (see p.21). This means that oxygen and carbon dioxide can move easily between the lungs and the blood supply.

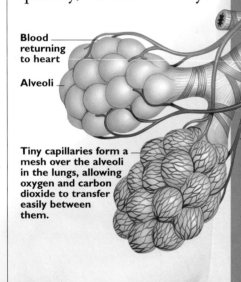

Blood returning to heart

Alveoli

Tiny capillaries form a mesh over the alveoli in the lungs, allowing oxygen and carbon dioxide to transfer easily between them.

Blood from heart

Trachea (windpipe)

Left lung

Heart

Cut surface of right lung

Bronchus

Diaphragm

Gas exchange
Blood arriving in the lungs from the heart is low in oxygen but high in carbon dioxide. Oxygen (O_2) passes into the red cell and carbon dioxide (CO_2) passes into the alveolus and is breathed out.

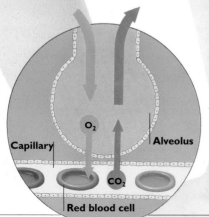

O_2

Capillary

Alveolus

CO_2

Red blood cell

Breathing tubes
You can feel the outside of your windpipe if you run a finger down the centre of your neck. It feels firm and ridged. This is because it has bands of cartilage in its wall helping to prevent it from damage in the event of any pressure on your neck. The trachea and bronchi also contain a small amount of muscle that makes the bore of the tube narrower when it is contracted. The smaller tubes, or bronchioles, and alveoli don't have any cartilage or muscle in their walls.

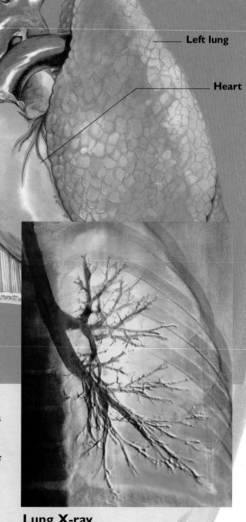

Lung X-ray
This bronchogram (see p.78) shows the branching supply of arteries in the lungs.

Breathing in and out

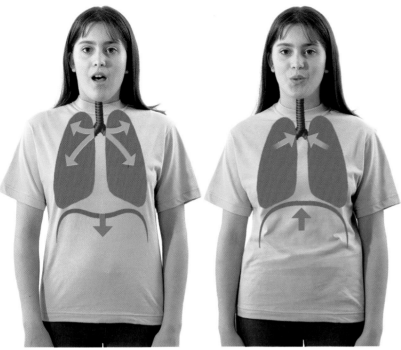

Breathing in
The diaphragm moves down and flattens, and the lungs fill with air.

Breathing out
The diaphragm moves up again, and air leaves the lungs.

How do you breathe in and out?

Your curved ribs are attached to your spine at the back, and your breast bone at the front. All the ribs are joined together by muscles. This is the rib cage, and one large muscle called the diaphragm forms its floor. When the rib muscles contract, the diaphragm moves down and the ribcage opens up rather like a bellows, sucking air into the lungs. When the diaphragm relaxes, it becomes a dome shape, and air is pushed out of the lungs again.

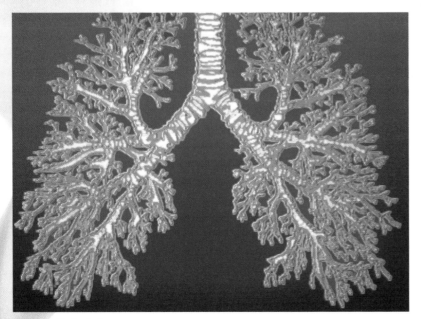

Tree of air tubes
This resin cast shows the tree-like structure of the airways in the two lungs.

HELPING AND HEALING

Asthma

Many people suffer from asthma. It occurs when the air tubes get narrower and their lining becomes swollen, producing more mucus than normal. This causes wheezy breathing, and a cough. Sometimes, asthma runs in the family, or it is related to an allergy (see p.29). In some people, a cause cannot be found. Inhalers work by reducing the mucus, and relaxing the muscle in the airways, allowing them to open again for easier breathing.

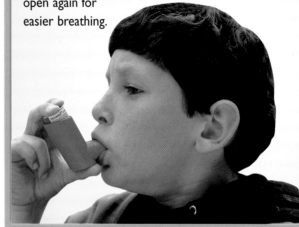

DID YOU KNOW?

Baby breaths
Babies breathe very fast, often around 25 times a minute. This slows down so that an average adult breathes only 15 times a minute.

Getting started
In the womb a baby makes breathing movements, but doesn't take its first full breath until it is born.

Smoke alarm
Cigarettes damage the hair cells lining your air tubes, so that you cannot easily filter the air you breathe.

Healthy lungs
Healthy lungs (see right) appear pink under the microscope. Pollution can blacken them, as shown below. Certain chemicals in cigarette smoke can permanently damage your lungs.

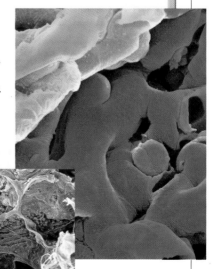

Eating

Most people enjoy eating, and mealtimes are often sociable occasions. The food you eat comes in many shapes, colours and textures. It can be combined and cooked to provide a wide range of meals and flavours. Your body is like an engine that needs topping up with fuel at regular intervals which is why most of us eat several times a day.

Why do you need food?

The most important reason for eating is that food provides you with energy. The energy content of food is measured in calories. Children and young adults need about 2000 calories a day. The more active you are, the more calories you need and while you're growing, you will need more calories than adults or elderly people. Food also provides you with water and essential nutrients that allow your organs to grow and develop. These nutrients include carbohydrates, fats, proteins, vitamins and minerals.

How does your food go down?

Once you have swallowed some food, rhythmic muscular contractions help to propel the food through your digestive system from your oesophagus to your anus. This is called peristalsis and it is triggered when food stretches the walls of your intestine.

Muscular contraction

Food

Intestine

Peristalsis

In this diagram you can see how the wall of the intestine contracts behind the food, and relaxes in front of it, pushing the food along in the direction of the arrow.

A healthy two-day diet

Eating well

To provide you with the correct mix of nutrients and water, you need to eat a variety of foods. This extraordinary hamburger is an example of the amount and type of food that you need to eat over a two-day period.

Fruit

Fruit provides fibre, which is is an essential part of your diet. Plenty of fibre helps to lower your risk of cancer of the colon and heart disease. Fruit is also a good source of vitamins and minerals and provides some energy.

Bread and pasta

These foods should be your main source of carbohydrate and fibre, providing energy and some vitamins and minerals. Sweets and cakes also provide energy. Cakes contain a lot of fat, also a source of energy. But keep your fat intake to less than a third of your daily calorie needs. More than that may be bad for your health.

Vegetables

Vegetables are a good source of fibre, vitamins and minerals, vital to the maintenance of your body. Only vitamins K and D are formed in your body. All the rest (vitamins A, B, C, and E) must come from your food. With a balanced diet, you are likely to be receiving the correct amount of vitamins and minerals.

Meat, fish, eggs, cheese

These foods provide protein, which should form about a sixth of your daily calorie intake. Protein is used to build and repair cells. Meat, fish, cheese and nuts contain lots of protein. Cheese, butter, oil, eggs, cakes and biscuits all have a high fat content.

How long does food take to digest?

Imagine you've just eaten a ham salad sandwich followed by an apple. The whole meal takes about a day to pass through your digestive system. The time it takes varies from person to person, sometimes taking 2 or 3 days. This meal provides you with 28 grams of protein, 46 grams of carbohydrate, 25 grams of fat, 5 grams of fibre, and about 520 calories of energy in all.

Mouth
Each mouthful of food spends about 15 seconds in your mouth.

Oesophagus
Once swallowed, it takes a couple of seconds for the mouthful to travel down your oesophagus to reach your stomach.

Stomach
Food stays in the stomach for 2-4 hours.

Small intestine
Passing through the small intestine takes 1-4 hours.

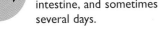

Large intestine
It takes at least 10 hours to pass through the large intestine, and sometimes several days.

DID YOU KNOW?

Energy levels
When you ride your bike for one hour, you use the same amount of energy as you need for four hours of bowling, or nine hours of homework!

Energy foods
Twelve French fries give you the same amount of energy as seven carrots, or five tangerines, or 33 sticks of celery.

The organs of digestion

As you chew food, saliva from the salivary glands squirts into your mouth. Saliva contains chemicals that start to digest the food. Swallowed food travels down the oesophagus into the stomach, where digestion continues. Food leaves the stomach and enters the small intestine, where juices from the pancreas and gallbladder help to digest food further.

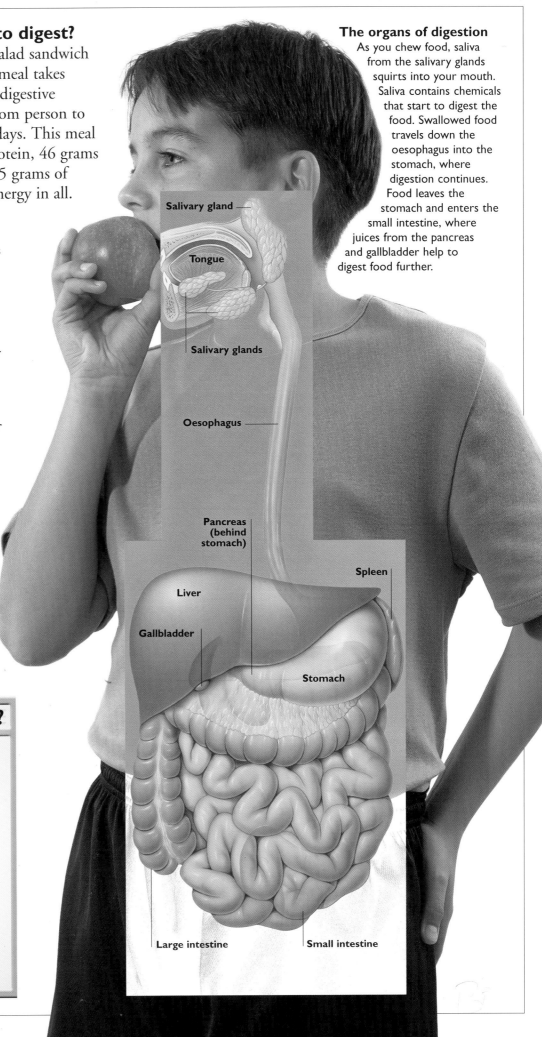

Salivary gland

Tongue

Salivary glands

Oesophagus

Pancreas (behind stomach)

Spleen

Liver

Gallbladder

Stomach

Large intestine

Small intestine

Digesting

The food and drink that you put in your mouth are chewed or churned about, and then swallowed. Your meal has now begun its journey through your digestive tract – a neatly packed tube about 7 metres in length from one end to the other. Along the way, chemicals, known as digestive enzymes, are squirted in. These enzymes split the food and drink into the basic raw materials, or nutrients, that your body needs. The nutrients are absorbed through the wall of the intestine into the bloodstream and are then used by your body. The parts of the food that you cannot use pass through your intestines.

What happens when you chew food?

You have sharp teeth at the front of your mouth for cutting food and larger teeth at the back for grinding it into pieces (see p.10). Ground up food is moved around your mouth by your tongue and mixed with saliva, which contains digestive enzymes, before being swallowed.

TRY IT YOURSELF

Salivary glands

Your digestive juices are produced automatically when food is present in your mouth. You can produce saliva just by looking at food. This is known as 'making your mouth water'. Try eating something with a sharp taste, like a slice of lemon tart. You should feel saliva in your mouth immediately.

How is food digested?

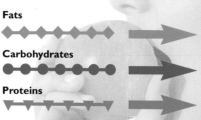

Fats

Carbohydrates

Proteins

Mouth

Food is mixed with saliva in your mouth. Saliva contains an enzyme that starts breaking down carbohydrate. The food and drink pass down a tube called the oesophagus, arriving in your stomach seconds later.

Stomach

The lining of your stomach produces acid and an enzyme, pepsin. The acid destroys any germs in your food and drink, and the pepsin begins to digest the proteins in your food. The semi-digested food passes into the first part of your small intestine, the duodenum.

Duodenum

Bile made by the liver and stored in the gallbladder is squirted into your duodenum, where it mixes with fat. It acts like a detergent on the fat globules, making them dissolve. The fat is then more easily digested by lipase, an enzyme squirted into your duodenum by the pancreas.

Small intestine

More enzymes, made by the pancreas (such as trypsin) and by the walls of the small intestine, complete the breakdown of proteins, carbohydrates and fats. Farther down your small intestine, these nutrients are absorbed into your bloodstream and taken to your liver, where they are stored or sent to the rest of the body. Bile is also absorbed here and returned to the liver.

Large intestine

Anything not absorbed from your small intestine travels into your large intestine. There, water is absorbed into your bloodstream. Everything else passes out of your body.

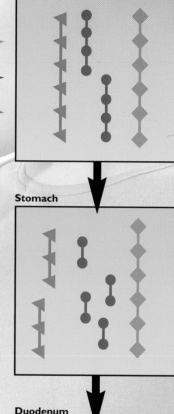

Mouth

Stomach

Duodenum

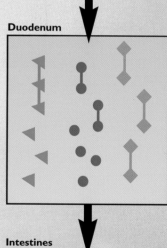

Intestines

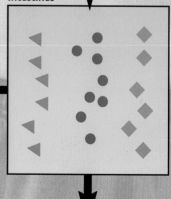

Nutrients into bloodstream

Waste out of body

How is food absorbed into the bloodstream?

The inside of your small intestine is folded into millions of small fronds, each one called a villus. These fronds increase the area of the inside of your small intestine, so that if it was laid out flat it would be about the size of a tennis court. Once your food has been fully digested, the nutrients are absorbed from your intestine into the blood vessels which flow through each villus.

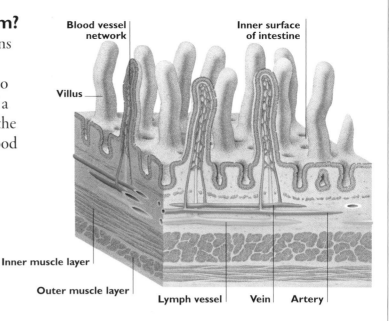

Blood vessel network

Inner surface of intestine

Villus

Inner muscle layer

Outer muscle layer

Lymph vessel   Vein   Artery

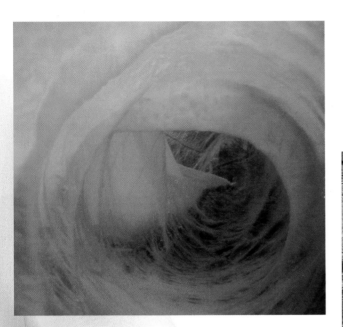

Small intestine
Your small intestine is about 5 metres long and is the part of your digestive system in which nutrients are absorbed into the bloodstream. The photograph of it (above) was taken through an endoscope (viewing tube) passed down the oesophagus and then through the stomach.

Villi
The lining of the small intestine has millions of tiny finger-like projections sticking out from it, called villi. Each contains a network of blood vessels. Nutrients are absorbed mainly through these villi. On the left is a microscope image of a cross-section through the intestinal lining, showing some villi.

Colon
The largest part of your large intestine is sometimes called the colon, seen here as the brown region in the X-ray. Within the colon, water is removed from the waste products of digestion. The waste products are moved along until they reach the final part of the large intestine, the rectum. When this is full, the waste products are expelled.

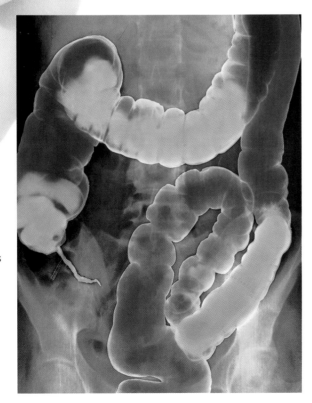

What are faeces?

The leftovers of food that you eat that cannot be digested pass right through your intestines and out the other end. This waste is known as faeces. Faeces are about three-quarters water, the rest is mainly undigested plant fibres and germs. The germs come from your large intestine, where they play an important role in helping to finish the digestion of any remaining food, often producing some smelly gases, such as methane and hydrogen sulphide. The germs also produce some vitamins. These germs are harmless as long as they do not spread to the rest of your body.

The brown colour of your faeces comes from the bile that is produced by your liver and squirted into your small intestine where it helps to digest fat. When the rectum is full of faeces, it has to be emptied.

Processing Waste

Your body, like any other machine, produces wastes. These collect in your large intestine and in your blood. To remain healthy, these wastes have to be disposed of. The main task of your kidneys is to filter your blood, removing the wastes from it.

How do your kidneys process waste?

You have a pair of kidneys, each about the size of your fist. They are located on either side of the backbone, just above waist level. Around 1.3 litres of blood pass through your kidneys every minute. This blood is filtered by the kidneys, so that any chemicals you don't need or are harmful to you are removed. The wastes form a solution mixed with water, called urine. From your kidneys, urine passes down tubes called ureters to the bladder, where it is stored until you are ready to go to the toilet.

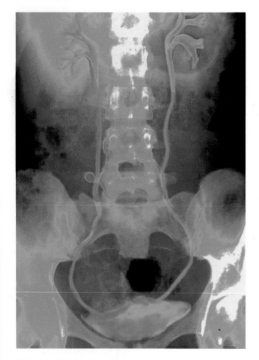

The urinary system
In this special X-ray called a urogram (see p.78), the kidneys are the pale blue areas at the top, either side of the column of spinal bones. The flower-like region, coloured green, within each kidney is the kidney pelvis. Urine collects in each pelvis before flowing down the ureters (seen here as two thin, winding tubes). The pale green area at the bottom of the X-ray is urine collecting in the bladder.

KEEPING HEALTHY

Testing urine

You may be asked to provide a sample of your urine when you visit the doctor for a check up or if you are unwell. This can be tested using a special test dipstick. Changes in colour indicate the presence of certain chemicals not normally present in your urine, such as glucose. The presence of glucose in your urine may appear if the level in your blood is unusually high, which happens in a condition called diabetes.

Sometimes your doctor will ask you to collect samples of your urine over a 24-hour period. This allows the doctor to test the amount of a chemical excreted in your urine, which may help to decide if you have kidney damage.

What else do your kidneys do?

Your kidneys also regulate your body's water content. When you exercise, or are in a hot climate, you lose water through your skin in sweat. If you don't drink enough to replace the lost water, your kidneys will try to conserve the water in your body by producing concentrated, dark yellow urine. On the other hand, if you drink more than you need, your kidneys will produce lots of dilute, pale yellow urine. Your kidneys also produce substances that control blood pressure and regulate your body's production of red blood cells.

HELPING AND HEALING

Kidney dialysis

If your kidneys stop working properly, you will gradually develop a build-up of waste chemicals in your blood, and will not be able to keep the correct balance of water in your body. Fortunately, these problems can be dealt with by using a dialysis machine, which mimics the action of your kidneys.

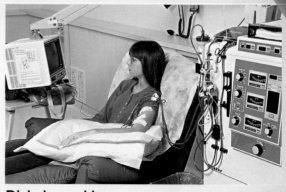

Dialysis machine
During a dialysis session you may have to be attached to the dialysis machine for several hours.

How do you know when to empty your bladder?

When your bladder is full, nerves in the wall of the bladder send messages to your brain, signalling discomfort. If you respond to the signal, you will go to the toilet to urinate. If you ignore the message, your bladder will continue to fill, until you become desperate to go to the toilet. However, you can usually control the opening of your bladder, even when you are asleep, so that you do not have an accident. This control is learnt as a child – before then, you will urinate whenever your bladder is full, regardless of where you are.

Why do you get thirsty?
Without water you would soon die. But how do you know when to drink? Within a part of your brain called the hypothalamus is a small region called the thirst centre. You know that if you eat something salty, you feel thirsty. This is because the thirst centre monitors the salt levels in your blood. If high, it sends signals to your brain to encourage you to get a drink and to your kidneys telling them to retain water. If salt levels fall too low, your thirst centre switches off the desire to drink, and your kidneys start to produce more dilute urine.

How do the kidneys work?
Each kidney (left) contains many tiny structures called nephrons. Each nephron (below) contains a wiggly pipe called a tubule, around which wrap several capillaries (see p.21). Blood flows into the glomerulus. From there, much of the water and many chemicals in the blood enter the tubule (blue arrows) and flow down it. Useful chemicals and some water are reabsorbed from the tubule back into the blood capillaries (green arrows), while the rest forms urine (orange arrows).

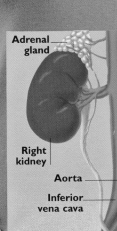

Adrenal gland
Urine collecting ducts
Renal artery
Right kidney
Left kidney
Aorta
Renal vein
Inferior vena cava
Ureter
Ureter
Bladder
Pelvis of kidney
Cortex, containing glomeruli of nephrons

A nephron
Capillary
Urine-collecting duct
Arteriole
Glomerulus
Tubule
Reabsorption

Hormones

Your hormones are chemicals produced and stored in various parts of your body. When required, a hormone is released into the bloodstream, and transported to its destination. Hormones control many important aspects of your body, including growth and energy levels, as well as regulating the level of certain chemicals, such as glucose and calcium, in your blood.

Pineal gland
The pineal gland produces the hormone melatonin, which helps to control your pattern of sleeping and waking.

Thyroid gland
The thyroid gland produces thyroxine, which helps control growth and energy production in the body.

Parathyroid glands
There are four parathyroid glands at the back of the thyroid gland. They produce parathyroid hormone, which helps to regulate the level of the mineral calcium in the body.

Adrenal glands
These two glands produce the hormones noradrenaline and adrenaline, which are released when your body is stressed (see p.49). They also produce the hormones aldosterone and cortisol, which control blood pressure. Cortisol also maintains the body's energy levels.

Pancreas
The pancreas produces insulin and glucagon, which adjust sugar (glucose) levels in the blood (see p.39).

Testes
The testes produce male sex hormones (mainly testosterone), which stimulate the production of sperm and are important at puberty in boys (see p.76).

Where are my hormones produced?
Organs that produce hormones are known as hormonal glands. The main ones include the pituitary, the thyroid, the adrenal glands and the pancreas, as well as a woman's ovaries and a man's testes. Some hormones are produced by organs whose main function has nothing to do with hormone production. For example, renin and erythropoietin are produced in the kidneys, whose main function is to remove waste products from the bloodstream.

Pituitary gland
The pituitary gland produces, amongst others, hormones that stimulate growth (growth hormone), milk production in breast feeding (prolactin and oxytocin), and release of the hormone thyroxine from the thyroid gland (thyroid-stimulating hormone). The pituitary also produces FSH (follicle-stimulating hormone), which stimulates a woman's ovaries to produce eggs. FSH also stimulates the testes in a man to secrete the male hormone testosterone and to produce sperm.

Kidneys
The kidneys produce erythropoietin, which stimulates the production of red blood cells, and renin, which helps to control blood pressure.

Ovaries
The ovaries (above) produce oestrogen and progesterone, which help control the production of an egg each month. Oestrogen levels increase at puberty (see p.76).

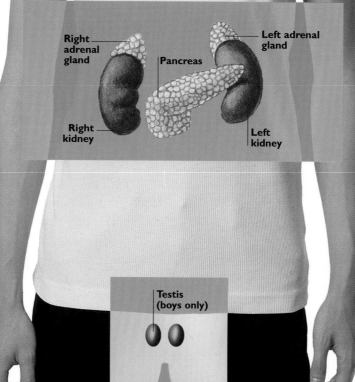

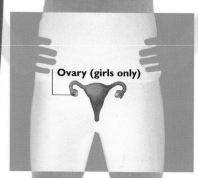

When are hormones produced?

Some glands produce hormones continuously. For example, the amount of the hormone thyroxine produced by the thyroid gland hardly varies from day to day. In contrast, the pituitary produces pulses of FSH (follicle-stimulating hormone) about every 2 hours. A woman's ovaries produce varying amounts of oestrogen and progesterone at different times of the month, usually in a pattern that repeats every month. Some hormones have a shorter repeating pattern. An example is cortisol, production of which is high in the early morning and low overnight. Growth hormone and prolactin levels are highest while you sleep. Many hormone levels rise if you are stressed.

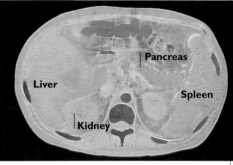

Thyroid scan
The activity of the thyroid gland can be monitored by a scanning technique called scintigraphy. In the scan shown to the left, the thyroid can be seen as the orange areas against the blue background.

Pancreas scan
One way of viewing the pancreas is with a CT scan (see p.78). This CT scan (right) shows a slice through the middle of the torso. The view is looking upward through the body.

Pancreas
Liver
Spleen
Kidney

Feedback mechanisms

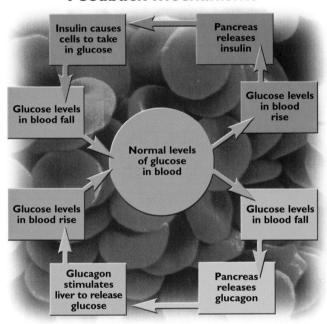

Insulin causes cells to take in glucose

Pancreas releases insulin

Glucose levels in blood fall

Glucose levels in blood rise

Normal levels of glucose in blood

Glucose levels in blood rise

Glucose levels in blood fall

Glucagon stimulates liver to release glucose

Pancreas releases glucagon

Regulating blood glucose levels
The level of glucose in your blood is regulated by feedback mechanisms (above). If glucose levels in your blood rise, your pancreas releases insulin, which moves the glucose into cells. If glucose levels fall, your pancreas secretes glucagon, which stimulates the release of more glucose from the liver. If the level of glucose in your blood is measured, it can be seen to fluctuate over time (below), but because of the feedback mechanisms, the level normally does not stray far from the average.

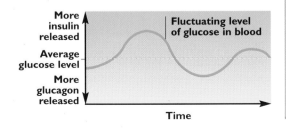

More insulin released
Average glucose level
More glucagon released

Fluctuating level of glucose in blood

Time

How do your hormones work?

Each hormone is released from its stores when the blood level of a particular chemical changes from its normal, average value. For example, after a meal, the level of the sugar glucose in your blood rises. This rise stimulates the pancreas to release a hormone called insulin into the bloodstream. Insulin is required to make your organs take up glucose from the blood and use it for energy.

If you are very active, your muscles need a large supply of glucose, and after a while the blood sugar level falls. This fall in blood glucose stimulates the pancreas to release another hormone, glucagon, into the bloodstream. Glucagon travels to the liver where it switches on the release of more glucose from stores.

HELPING AND HEALING

Diabetes

Diabetes is a condition in which the blood contains abnormally high levels of glucose. In many cases this is because the pancreas produces insufficient insulin. Children with diabetes usually have to inject themselves with insulin several times a day. This helps to control the level of glucose in their blood and allows them to live near-normal lives. Devices called injection pens, which are preloaded with insulin cartridges, provide a convenient method for injecting the hormone.

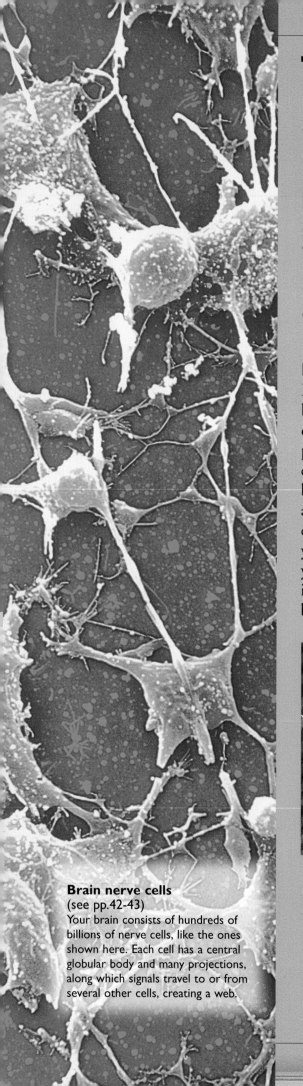

The Control System

YOUR BODY IS AN EXTREMELY COMPLEX machine, controlled by your brain and spinal cord. Your amazing brain learns from experience and is capable of creative and original thought. This sophisticated system makes humans the most intelligent beings on earth.

Nerves

Fanning out from your brain and spinal cord in all directions are numerous cord-like projections called nerves. These are like electrical cables, carrying signals between your brain and spinal cord and the rest of the body. Some nerves carry signals from sense organs towards your brain, others carry instructions to your muscles, glands and organs. These instructions control movement and the body's internal functioning

Spinal cord

Synapses
(see p.45)
Where the branching ends of nerves meet a muscle, there are connections called synapses. Signals passing through the synapses cause muscles to contract or relax.

Brain nerve cells
(see pp.42-43)
Your brain consists of hundreds of billions of nerve cells, like the ones shown here. Each cell has a central globular body and many projections, along which signals travel to or from several other cells, creating a web.

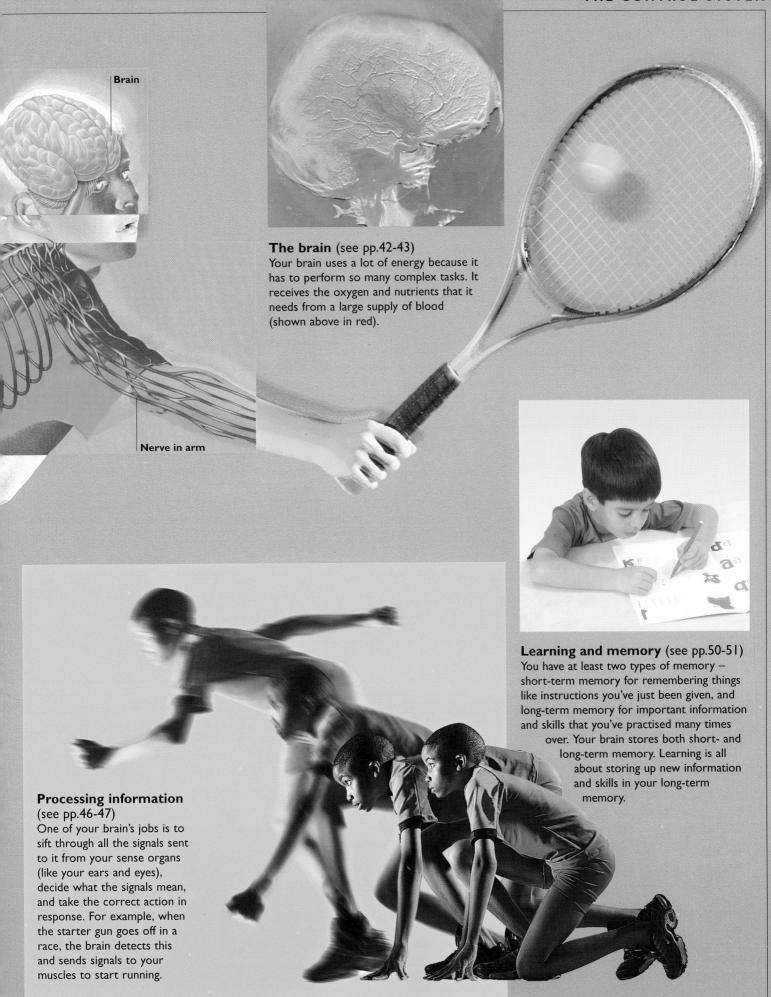

Brain

Nerve in arm

The brain (see pp.42-43)
Your brain uses a lot of energy because it has to perform so many complex tasks. It receives the oxygen and nutrients that it needs from a large supply of blood (shown above in red).

Learning and memory (see pp.50-51)
You have at least two types of memory – short-term memory for remembering things like instructions you've just been given, and long-term memory for important information and skills that you've practised many times over. Your brain stores both short- and long-term memory. Learning is all about storing up new information and skills in your long-term memory.

Processing information (see pp.46-47)
One of your brain's jobs is to sift through all the signals sent to it from your sense organs (like your ears and eyes), decide what the signals mean, and take the correct action in response. For example, when the starter gun goes off in a race, the brain detects this and sends signals to your muscles to start running.

The Brain

The brain is the control centre for your body. It contains around 100 billion nerve cells – about the same number as there are stars in our galaxy. You use your brain to perform hundreds of tasks, often at the same time. For example, you can imagine a picture, describe it and store the memory of it for years to come. At the same time you can feel, listen and see. Your brain absorbs your experiences and generates the unique ideas and thoughts that make up your personality.

What does your brain look like?

The surface of your brain, or cortex, is folded and looks like a large walnut, or a small cauliflower. It is divided into two halves, known as cerebral hemispheres, which are connected to each other. Each cerebral hemisphere is made up of several different lobes, which are named after the skull bones covering them. The cortex is crinkly because its millions of little folds increase the surface area.

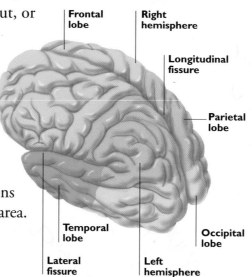

Frontal lobe

Right hemisphere

Longitudinal fissure

Parietal lobe

Temporal lobe

Occipital lobe

Lateral fissure

Left hemisphere

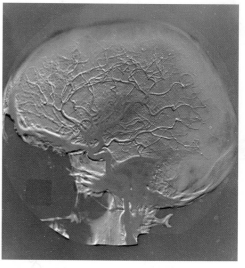

Blood supply

Because your brain is the control centre for your body it needs a big blood supply. All the small branches supplying the brain come from four big arteries in your neck. Your brain is very sensitive to a shortage of blood. If the blood supply to your brain is cut off for any reason, you lose consciousness in 10 seconds.

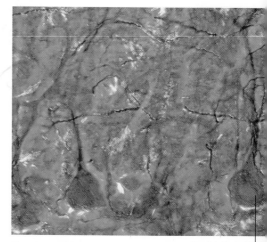

Brain cells
Purkinje cell

The cerebellum contains the largest nerve cells in the human body, known as Purkinje cells.

Grey and white matter

The grey part of your brain is the outer layer, or cortex. You use it for the most difficult mental tasks. The reason it looks grey is because it consists mainly of nerve cells. The white matter is the inner layer that is made from nerve fibres, or axons (see pp.44-45). These carry signals across the brain.

DID YOU KNOW?

Brain names
Many of the names given to parts of the body are Greek. The names sound complicated, but they are useful descriptions too. For example, cerebellum means little brain; cortex means bark or rind and thalamus means inner room.

Brain area
If the surface of the brain was unfolded and laid out flat, it would cover a bed.

Brain size
Men have bigger brains than women, but there is no link between size of brain and how clever you are.

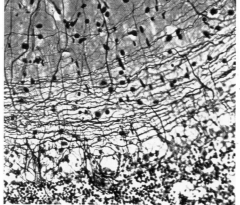

The cerebellum

Your cerebellum helps you to control your posture and balance, and it co-ordinates movements. This microscope image shows nerve cells and fibres within the organ.

White matter is the inner layer

Grey matter is the outer layer, or cortex

What is inside your brain?

From a cross-section of the brain you can see that the surface, or cortex, surrounds several other structures. Each part of the brain has a special function, but the parts work together in a team. The corpus callosum, for example, connects the two cerebral hemispheres with around 200 million nerve fibres. Nearer the spinal cord is the brain stem. It is made up of the medulla, midbrain and pons, and it keeps your lungs breathing and your heart beating. It also contains millions of nerve cells that connect the brain to the rest of the body.

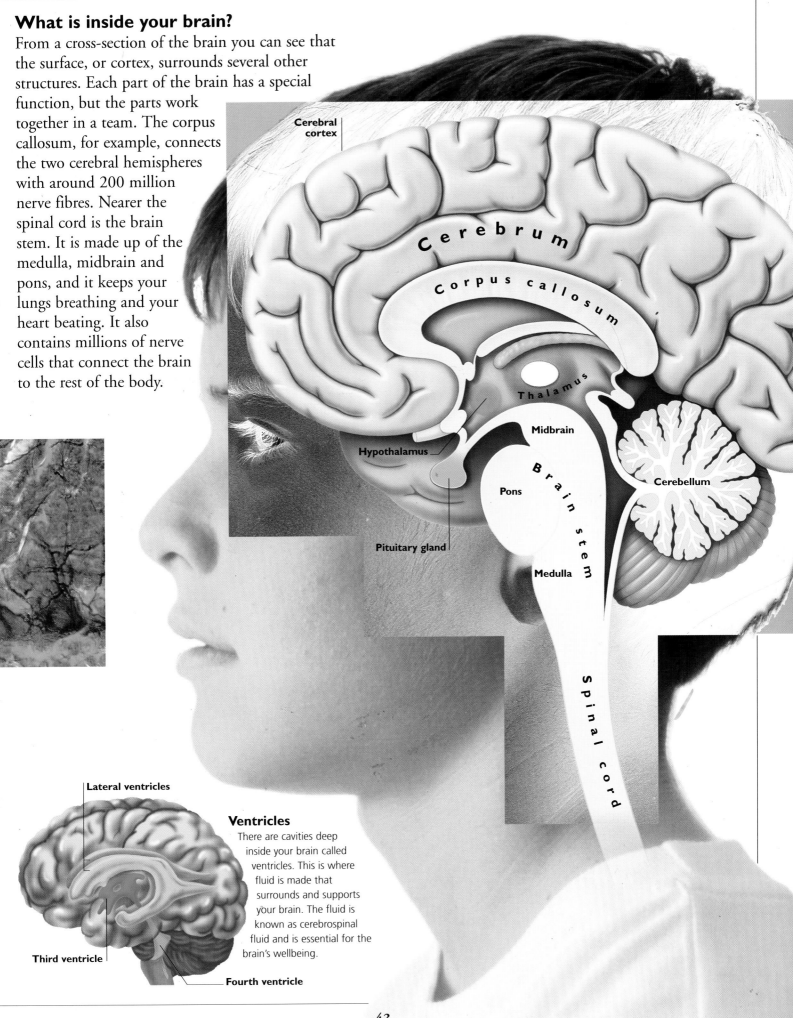

Cerebral cortex

Cerebrum

Corpus callosum

Thalamus

Midbrain

Hypothalamus

Cerebellum

Pons

Brain stem

Pituitary gland

Medulla

Spinal cord

Lateral ventricles

Third ventricle

Fourth ventricle

Ventricles

There are cavities deep inside your brain called ventricles. This is where fluid is made that surrounds and supports your brain. The fluid is known as cerebrospinal fluid and is essential for the brain's wellbeing.

43

The Nervous System

Your nervous system is more powerful and versatile than any computer. It is capable of carrying out many complex tasks at the same time. While you are reading this, your nervous system is controlling your eye movements, as well as regulating your breathing, your digestive system and the speed at which your heart beats. Most of the time these processes are going on without you being aware, but the nervous system also controls all of your deliberate actions whether you're hitting a tennis ball, threading a needle, or scratching an itchy spot.

What parts does the nervous system have?

Your nervous system has two main parts: the central nervous system (CNS) and the peripheral nervous system. The CNS includes the brain and spinal cord and is your body's control centre. Some peripheral nerves carry messages from the CNS to the rest of the body. These are known as motor nerves because they are responsible for doing and moving. Other peripheral nerves carry messages from the body toward the brain. These are known as sensory nerves because the signals they carry come from your sense organs and receptors (see pp.54-61).

Protecting the central nervous system

Your brain is soft and could be damaged easily if it was not protected inside your skull. The spinal cord is enclosed by the vertebral bones that link together to form the spine.

Brain

Skull

Spinal cord
Vertebra

Spinal nerve

Spinal cord

Vertebra

Ulnar nerve

Spinal cord

Radial nerve

Brain

How do nerves carry messages?

Electrical impulses pass along the nerves, carrying messages to and from the brain. Many nerve fibres are coated in a fatty substance called myelin, which increases the speed of the electrical signal. Each nerve forms a connection with a muscle, or a gland or another nerve. This junction is known as a synapse (see below) and it ensures messages are passed to the right destination.

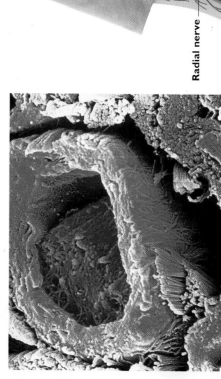

Bundle of nerve fibres
In this image, the red fibres in the centre are nerve fibres, surrounded by a sheath (in blue), making one bundle, or fascicle. The connective tissue is in green

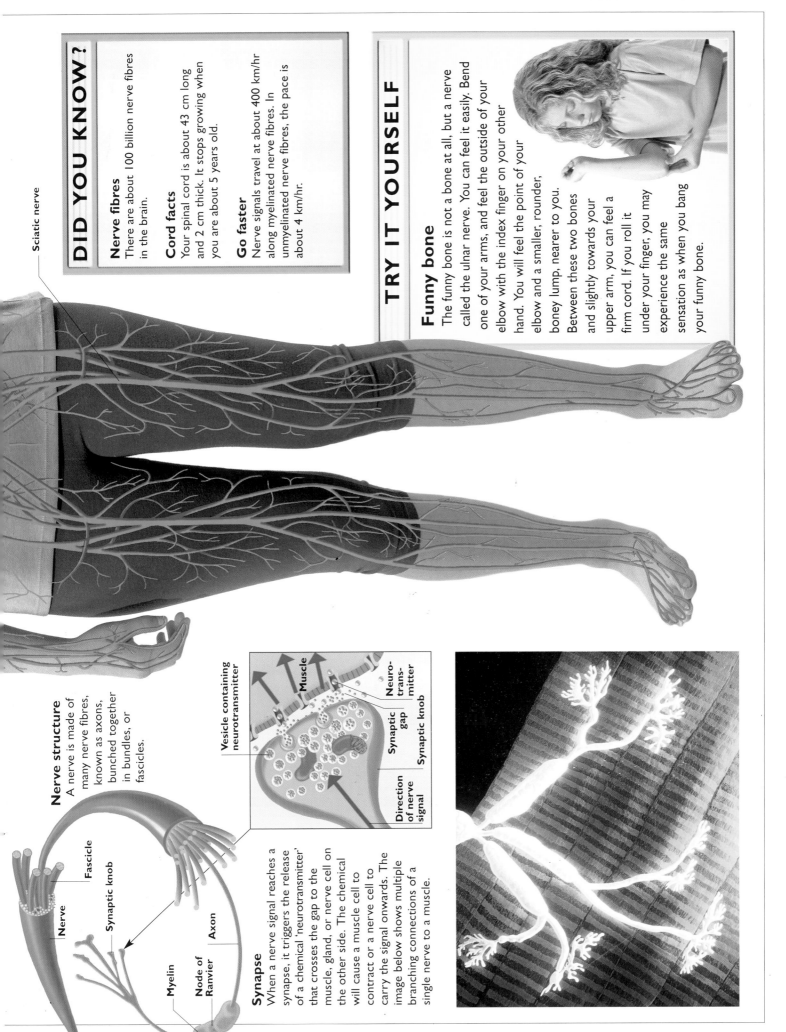

Sciatic nerve

TRY IT YOURSELF

Funny bone
The funny bone is not a bone at all, but a nerve called the ulnar nerve. You can feel it easily. Bend one of your arms, and feel the outside of your elbow with the index finger on your other hand. You will feel the point of your elbow and a smaller, rounder, boney lump, nearer to you. Between these two bones and slightly towards your upper arm, you can feel a firm cord. If you roll it under your finger, you may experience the same sensation as when you bang your funny bone.

Nerve structure
A nerve is made of many nerve fibres, known as axons, bunched together in bundles, or fascicles.

Fascicle

Synaptic knob

Nerve

Myelin

Node of Ranvier

Axon

Synapse
When a nerve signal reaches a synapse, it triggers the release of a chemical 'neurotransmitter' that crosses the gap to the muscle, gland, or nerve cell on the other side. The chemical will cause a muscle cell to contract or a nerve cell to carry the signal onwards. The image below shows multiple branching connections of a single nerve to a muscle.

Vesicle containing neurotransmitter

Muscle

Neuro-transmitter

Synaptic gap

Synaptic knob

Direction of nerve signal

45

Processing Information

Millions of electrical signals arrive in your brain every second, carrying information gathered by your body from the world around you. Your brain's job is to decide what the signals mean, and whether or not they are useful. Many of the messages passed between the nerve cells in your brain are involved in planning and controlling movement. Others are important for generating ideas or making decisions. But perhaps the brain's hardest job is to understand itself. We know a lot about how it works, but there is still much more to know.

How does your brain make a part of your body move?

When you have to do a difficult task, you probably think about how you are going to do it before you start. Your brain is the same. The planning process takes place in a split second in several parts of your brain, including the cerebellum and the premotor cortex. From there, messages are sent to the motor cortex, a part of the brain that controls your muscles. Commands from the motor cortex are relayed as electrical signals down your spinal cord to the nerves that supply the muscles, which then signal the muscles to contract.

Tying shoe laces
What seems like a simple task, such as bending over to tie a shoe lace, is a complex undertaking for your brain. Try it now, making a list of what movements are needed. Your list probably includes bending your waist and knees, moving your back, neck, arms, hands and eyes, and complex movements of your fingers. Each of these body parts is controlled by many muscles. The whole process involves hundreds of muscles.

How does your brain adjust and control movement?

As your body moves, sensors in your tendons, joints, skin and inner ear detect detailed information about changes in the position of your body, and send messages along sensory nerves back to the motor cortex. This information allows the motor cortex to compare the commands it made with the actual movements achieved, and so make any adjustments required. Moving your fingers or tongue involves many muscles, and the movements need to be skilled and fine, so large areas of the motor cortex are devoted to controlling these muscles.

Messages from the brain pass along motor nerves, causing muscles to contract and bring about motion. Here, the dark green arrows show the route of messages going to muscles in the hands.

Sensory messages sent back to the brain provide information about movements that have taken place. Here, the light green arrows indicate messages from receptors in the wrists. This 'feedback' helps the brain to make the movement smooth.

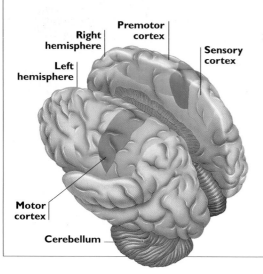

Right hemisphere

Premotor cortex

Sensory cortex

Left hemisphere

Motor cortex

Cerebellum

How fast can you react?

When the starter gun goes off in a race, a message is sent along nerves from your ears to your brain. Your brain registers the information it receives and recognises it as a signal from a starter gun. It sends a message to your muscles to start running. The time it takes all of this to happen is known as your reaction time. A typical reaction time is about 0.25 seconds.

TRY IT YOURSELF

Perception

Your brain constantly tries to make sense of the information it receives from your sense organs. This process is known as 'perception'. Sometimes the brain comes up with two alternative ways of interpretating the same information. For example, look at the picture on the right. Do you see an old hag, or a young woman turning her head away from you? You may eventually see both, though not at the same time.

How does your brain handle language?

Your brain has two halves, or hemispheres. Language is generally handled in one side of your brain, called the dominant hemisphere, which in most people is the left hemisphere. The dominant hemisphere contains two regions, called Wernicke's area and Broca's area, that play important roles in speech and language. Wernicke's area is involved in planning what you are going to say. It sends this information to Broca's area, where the information is turned into detailed instructions for movement of muscles in the lips, tongue and larynx (or voice box). These instructions are sent to the appropriate parts of the motor cortex, which sends signals to the muscles.

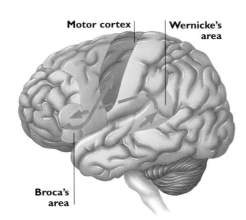

Motor cortex | Wernicke's area

Broca's area

Processing speech in the brain
In this diagram you can see that the words you say start in Wernicke's area, which plans the sounds. The arrows indicate the flow of nerve signals, through Broca's area and finally to the motor cortex.

Which half of your brain is more important?

Both halves of your brain have important functions. Although the 'dominant' hemisphere is more important for language and manual skills, the other half is important for recognising objects, faces, and music. Both halves are involved in planning and controlling movement. The left side of the motor cortex controls muscles on the right side of your body, and vice versa.

DID YOU KNOW?

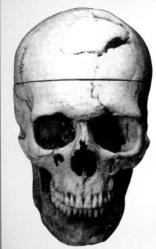

Personality

In 1848, an American railway worker called Phineas Gage had a terrible accident. A steel bar plunged into his skull (see left), destroying the frontal lobes of his brain. He recovered, but his personality changed completely. Research has since confirmed that the frontal lobes of your brain influence your personality and behaviour.

IQ

IQ stands for 'Intelligence Quotient'. It is found by dividing your mental age (established through a series of tests) by your actual age and multiplying the result by 100. For example, if a 10-year-old boy has a mental age of 12, his IQ is (12/10) x 100 = 120. If on the other hand he has a mental age of 8, his IQ is 80. About three-quarters of people have an IQ between 80 and 120.

The Automatic Body

Imagine you are sitting quietly in the shade, reading a book. Your eyes move along the lines of text, your hands turn the pages. These are voluntary movements, like stretching your arms, or pedalling a bike. You are aware of these actions, even though the messages are sent through the nervous system very fast. But while you are reading, your heart continues to beat, you carry on breathing and your intestines carry on digesting your last meal, all without you having to think about it. These tasks are performed automatically by nerves that form part of the autonomic nervous system.

How does the autonomic nervous system work?

There are two parts to the autonomic nervous system – the parasympathetic and the sympathetic. The parasympathetic nervous system is active when you are relaxed or resting. It helps your body conserve or restore energy, and its nerves connect with the heart and digestive organs.

The sympathetic nervous system has an opposite effect on your body. It is responsible for preparing you to face up to attack or danger. It is this system that gives you 'nerves' before performing in front of an audience, or sitting an exam. You probably know from experience that the right amount of nervous energy can make you perform better, but too much can make you panic.

Parasympathetic nerves
These send messages from the brain and from the lower part of the spinal cord.

Parasympathetic system

Saliva is produced.

Your heart beats at a steady pace.

Gallbladder squeezes its contents into the digestive system

Digestion of your last meal continues as you cycle along

Parasympathetic
While you are riding your bike using voluntary movements, the body's automatic functions, such as breathing and digesting, continue thanks to the parasympathetic nervous system.

Sleepy head
Without sleep, our minds and bodies slow down, our health deteriorates and we can suffer a degree of stress that could be fatal. We know that there are two kinds of sleep: REM (rapid eye movement) sleep when you dream, and non-REM sleep. Sleep is regulated by the parasympathetic nervous system, which helps restore energy to your body.

Sympathetic nerves
These come from the middle region of the spinal cord.

Your pupils will dilate, allowing more light in so you can see as much as possible.

Blood is diverted from your skin to your muscles where it is needed, so your face looks white.

Your heart beats harder and faster to increase the flow of blood to your muscles.

Your muscles receive more oxygen so that they can pedal faster, or squeeze the brakes hard.

Sympathetic system

Your liver releases high energy glucose into your bloodstream.

The muscle at the opening of your bladder is tightly closed to stop you urinating.

Sympathetic
Your sympathetic nervous system helps you to react when you are in danger. Imagine you are on your bike and a car pulls out in front of you. A sudden burst of activity in your sympathetic nervous system can save you.

Did it make you jump?
A shock in a scary film produces a surge of adrenaline that may make you jump as your body prepares for action.

KEEPING HEALTHY

Coping with nerves
Before performing in public, or taking a test, it is normal to feel a little nervous. The sensation of 'butterflies' happens when a lot of adrenaline is produced by your adrenal glands. Adrenaline usually helps you to perform well, but sometimes it can have the opposite effect, limiting your ability to do anything. This is the state of panic, and it is a nasty and frightening experience. You can prevent panic by learning some simple relaxation techniques:

• Start by closing your eyes.
• Think about your breathing. Imagine that each breath is a wave on the seashore, washing in and out.
• Every time you breathe in, count slowly to two.
• Every time you breathe out, count to four.
• Your breathing should become slow and rhythmic. After a few minutes, slowly open your eyes. You should feel calmer and more relaxed.

What is the 'flight or fight' reaction?
When you are in danger, your body produces a surge of adrenaline, a hormone from the adrenal glands. You have two adrenal glands, one on top of each of your kidneys. Adrenaline gives a burst of energy by increasing your heart rate and the amount of blood flowing to your organs. This lets you act quickly in a threatening situation – either by running away, or by facing up to it. This is known as the 'flight or fight' reaction.

Learning and Memory

Can you think of something you learned recently, like the words of a song or a new game? How many times did you have to practise it before you felt confident? Once? Twice? Or many times? When you are learning to do something, every time you do it, you use your memory of your previous experience to help you. If you don't practise for a week, you may remember only part of what you learned. But catching up is quicker each time. Once you have mastered it, your brain remembers the skill and stores it in your memory.

Focusing on the task
You will remember more, and learn faster, if you are working towards a goal, such as passing a test or receiving a reward. The more you concentrate on your task, the quicker you will learn and remember. It also helps if you enjoy the task and you receive praise for your efforts.

How do you learn?

Have you ever watched a scary video? Do you remember the first time you watched it? You can probably remember how scared you were. If you watch that video again, you will know what to expect, and you may react differently, perhaps by being a bit less scared because you have learned what to expect.

This is an example of how experience helps you to learn. There are many other ways to learn; we probably all use a combination of types at different times. Sometimes you learn by associating one thing with another, like lightning with thunder. Sometimes you learn by being told how to do something, although things often don't make sense until you've had a chance to do it for yourself. Often we learn simply through being inquisitive – if you are in a room with lots of interesting things in it, you will learn a lot by yourself.

2. The musician can save his best musical ideas in the computer's memory sytem. He can change them using a mouse or computer keyboard.

1. The musician can use the synthesiser keyboard to try out new ideas. These appear as sound waves or musical notes on the computer screen at the same time as he hears them.

DID YOU KNOW?

Memory filtering
You couldn't possibly remember everything – your brain would soon clog up. Instead it filters through your memories, storing only a proportion of them.

Blasts from the past
Sometimes the memory of something from the past is associated with a particular smell or sound, which will trigger the memory in your mind.

How does your memory work?

Scientists who study how the brain works think there are at least two different types of memory. Short-term memory is for information you've just been told, such as a phone number, or for recent events, such as what you had for lunch. It has a limited capacity and only lasts for a short time. For example, you may be able to remember what you had for dinner yesterday, but will you still be able to in a week? Important events and information, and skills or facts that you have learned by repetition, go into long-term memory. Your brain has an amazing long-term memory capacity – millions of different memories can be stored. These long-term memories will probably stay with you for ever.

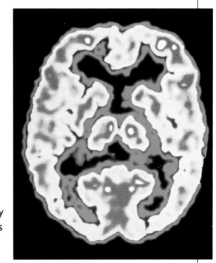

Mental activity in the brain

This image is a PET scan (see p.78) showing a cross-section of the brain of a person with normal memory and other mental functions. The red and yellow areas are regions of high brain activity. The blue and black regions are areas of lower or no activity.

Learning by experimentation

A lot of learning and creativity occurs through experimentation, by trying different ideas and seeing what works best. Here, a young musician is composing a piece of music on a synthesiser linked to a computer.

3. Later on, the musician can use his stored ideas to create a musical composition. Meanwhile, he is learning different steps and skills in using the computer programme.

KEEPING HEALTHY

Stimulating the mind

Although short-term memory ability declines as you get older, you can carry on learning new skills at any age. To learn, you need to keep an active mind. Reading, conversation, visiting new places, and playing games (even some computer games!) are all stimulating for the mind.

TRY IT YOURSELF

Mnemonics

It can help to link something you are trying to remember to an image in your mind, so that when you want to remember it, you have the picture to help you. Another trick is to use a mnemonic. The initial letters of a phrase can be useful for remembering something. For example: "Richard of York gave battle in vain" helps you to remember the colours of the rainbow: red, orange, yellow, green, blue, indigo and violet.

Tray game

Test your memory. Collect some items on a tray. Spend one minute looking at them, then cover the tray with a cloth. How many of the objects can you recall?

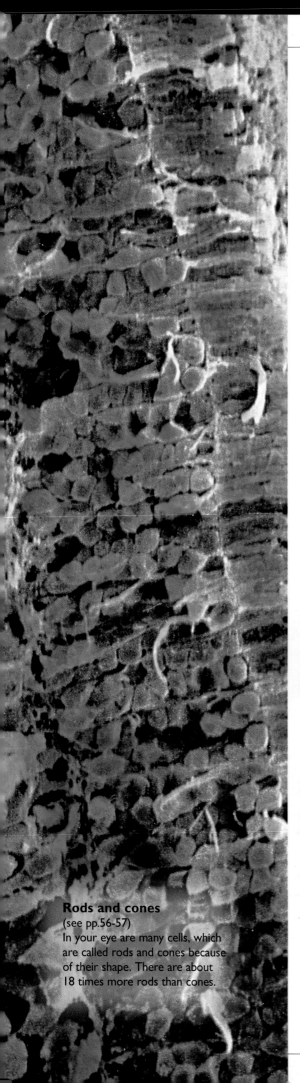

The Senses

SIGHT, HEARING, SMELL, TASTE AND TOUCH
are the five senses that link everyone to the
outside world. It is only through your senses that
you can smell a rose, taste a chocolate, hear a
friend on the phone or see a movie. But your
senses are not only there for pleasure, they also
help to protect you.

How the senses work
The sensations picked up by your
eyes, mouth and ears trigger
electrical impulses that travel along
the nerves to the brain, which
processes them. The largest sense
organ is your skin. Crammed full
of sensors, it records everything you
touch. Your senses of taste and
smell work together, one enhancing
the other. Meanwhile your eyes and
ears provide a steady flow of images
and sounds that enable you to see
and hear.

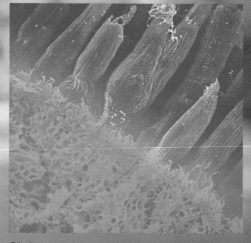

Sight (see pp.56-57)
This is a magnified image of rods and cones,
light sensitive cells in your eye that respond
to brightness, detail and colour.

Smell (see pp.60-61)
This highly magnified picture shows the cilia. These are hairs
in your nose that trigger nerve impulses when they come into
contact with a chemical that makes a scent or smell.

Rods and cones
(see pp.56-57)
In your eye are many cells, which
are called rods and cones because
of their shape. There are about
18 times more rods than cones.

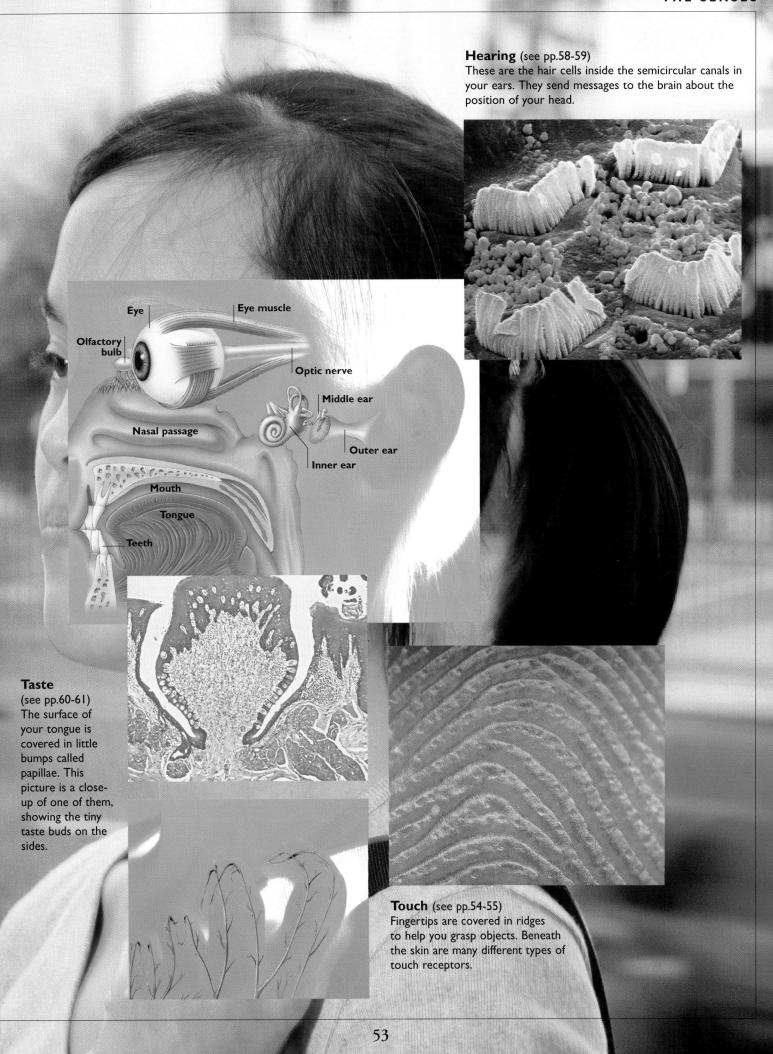

Hearing (see pp.58-59)
These are the hair cells inside the semicircular canals in your ears. They send messages to the brain about the position of your head.

Eye

Eye muscle

Olfactory bulb

Optic nerve

Middle ear

Nasal passage

Outer ear

Inner ear

Mouth

Tongue

Teeth

Taste
(see pp.60-61)
The surface of your tongue is covered in little bumps called papillae. This picture is a close-up of one of them, showing the tiny taste buds on the sides.

Touch (see pp.54-55)
Fingertips are covered in ridges to help you grasp objects. Beneath the skin are many different types of touch receptors.

53

Touch

As you are reading this, how much can you feel? You can probably feel the smooth paper of this book, and the sharper edge of the page. You may be able to feel the pressure of your body on a chair. Perhaps you can also feel that the air around you is warm, or maybe you are in a cold place. If you close your eyes and try to identify an object using your hands, millions of tiny sensors in your skin help you to tell the difference between cold and hot, soft and firm. You can also tell if something is dangerously sharp, or if it is vibrating. This sophisticated sense provides you with a continual flow of information about your immediate environment.

What are touch receptors?

Information about how an object feels is detected by millions of sensory nerve fibres, which have endings in your skin. Sensory nerves carry signals from your skin to your spinal cord and then to your brain. The nerve endings in the skin are able to detect touch, pressure, vibration, heat and cold. The nerve endings responsible for detecting deep pressure, vibration, and light touch have distinctive shapes and are known as receptors.

Fingertips and touch

Your fingertips are covered in ridged patterns (see below) which, by increasing friction, aid the finger's ability to grasp objects. Beneath the skin's surface are many different types of nerve endings and receptors involved in touch, listed below.

Free nerve endings
These are rather like the bare ends of a wire. They respond to touch, pressure and temperature and occur everywhere in your skin.

Merkel's disks
These consist of branching tufts of nerve endings at the base of the outer layer of skin (see p.8). They respond to light touch.

Meissner's corpuscles
These receptors are found just beneath the outer layer of the skin. They respond to light touch and pressure.

Ruffini's endings
These receptors are found below the outer layer of skin. They respond to touch and pressure.

Pacinian corpuscles
These relatively large, oval receptors are found deep down in the skin. They are found in the palms, soles, joints, and nipples, and detect vibration.

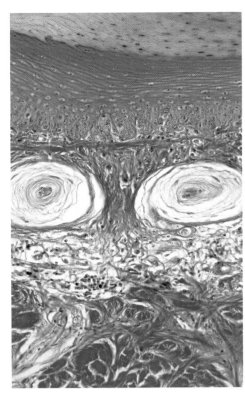

Pacinian corpuscles
The two oval-shaped bodies in this image are Pacinian corpuscles. Each consists of a nerve ending surrounded by layers of membranes, which make the receptors look like tiny onions. The red area is the top layer of skin.

Meissner corpuscle
The bean-shaped region in the lower part of this image is a Meissner corpuscle. These receptors help you to discriminate detail about an object, and so there are many of them in your hands and feet.

HELPING AND HEALING

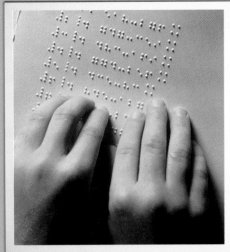

Braille
Louis Braille was a Frenchman who went blind when he was three. He invented a system of reading that relies on patterns of raised dots. Each pattern represents a letter of the alphabet. Using your fingers, you can feel the pattern of dots and read words. One hand reads the dots, while the other hand feels ahead for the next line.

Reading with touch
By using the sense of touch, you can read by feeling instead of using your eyes.

How do you feel pain?
Remember the last time you stubbed your toe? You may have shouted something, and perhaps you bent over to rub your toe, or sat down. This sequence of events starts with free nerve endings in the skin of your toe being stimulated by the sharp injury. Messages are sent along sensory nerves from your toe to your spinal cord. From there, messages pass along nerves to your muscles, which pull your foot away from where you stubbed it. At the same time, the message from the sensory nerve endings is sent to your brain.

Responding to pain
The pain signal is sent along nerves to the spine and triggers a reflex action. The reflex action makes muscles pull the leg away from the source of pain. The signal also reaches the brain, where it triggers the feeling of pain.

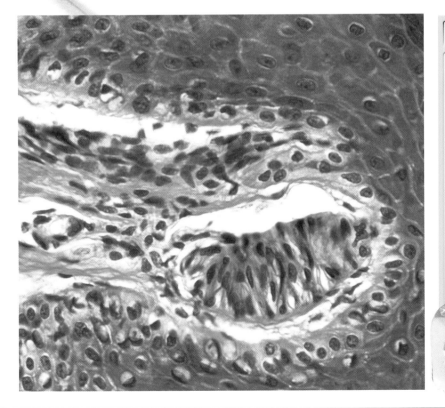

TRY IT YOURSELF

Skin sensitivity
Some parts of your body are more sensitive than others. You use your fingers to find out about the world around you, and in the tips of your fingers are thousands of touch receptors, packed into the skin. Your lips and tongue are also very sensitive to touch. Other body parts have very few touch receptors.

Try this experiment: Ask a friend to touch two areas of the bare skin on your back at the same time, using two feathers, or two ice cubes, a small distance apart. How far apart do the touched regions have to be before you can feel two feathers or two ice cubes? If you try the same experiment on a fingertip, you'll quickly see how much more sensitive your fingertip is than your back.

Sight

From babyhood your eyes provide you with a constant supply of detailed three-dimensional colour images of the world. Like a highly sophisticated video camera, your eyes take in thousands of images every day – many of which are stored in your memory for ever. Pictures sent to your brain from your eyes are combined with information from other senses and from other parts of the brain to give you a full understanding of what you can see.

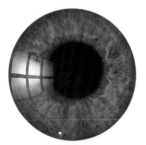

Pupil narrows in bright light

Pupil opens in dim light

What is inside your eye?

The eyeball is made up of three layers. The outer layer has two parts, the white sclera and the transparent cornea. The middle layer contains blood vessels, the coloured iris and the lens. The inner layer is the retina, which contains millions of light-sensitive cells, called rods and cones. The eye in front of the lens is filled with aqueous humour, a fluid containing oxygen, glucose and proteins. The rest of the eye contains vitreous humour, a clear gel that helps to keep the eye's shape.

A human eye

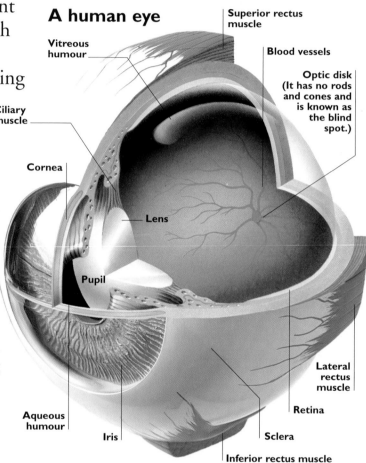

Vitreous humour
Superior rectus muscle
Blood vessels
Optic disk (It has no rods and cones and is known as the blind spot.)
Ciliary muscle
Cornea
Lens
Pupil
Lateral rectus muscle
Retina
Aqueous humour
Iris
Sclera
Inferior rectus muscle

The pupil

The pupil is the central black part of your eye that lets in light. Muscles in the iris (the coloured part) change the size of the pupil to regulate the amount of light that reaches the retina. Too much light is harmful, so in bright light the pupil gets smaller. In dim light the pupil widens to allow as much light as possible to enter the eye.

Tear gland

Tears are made in the lacrimal (tear) glands above each eye. When you blink, tears sweep across the surface of your eyeball, washing away dust and germs. Excess tears normally drain away through the tear ducts into the nose. When you feel emotional, nerves trigger your lacrimal glands to produce more tears. The increased flow of tears into the tear ducts gives you a runny nose, and tears will overflow from your eyes and roll down your cheeks.

Lacrimal (tear) gland
Tear ducts
Nasolacrimal sac

How do you see?

When you look at an object, light rays travel from it through the pupil. The lens focuses and bends the rays to make a clear, but upside-down image on the retina. The retina has light-sensitive cells that send electrical signals along the optic nerve to the brain. The brain interprets the information it receives and turns the image the right way up so that you can understand the shape, size and colour of the object.

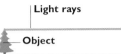

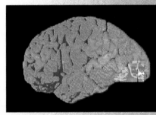

Blood vessel
Image focused on retina
Pupil
Lens
Retina
Optic nerve

Seeing objects in 3D

Light from some parts of your field of view (the pink areas in this diagram) falls on the left sides of the retinas in your eyes. Information about these areas goes to the left visual cortex (pink) at the back of the brain. Information about other areas (blue) goes to the right visual cortex. Information about any object in the lilac area (where pink and blue overlap) goes to both sides of the visual cortex. This helps judge distance to an object in the lilac area, and the object is seen in 3-dimensions.

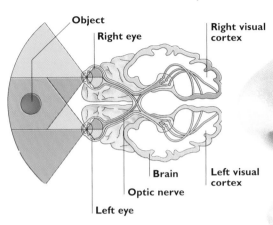

Object
Right eye
Right visual cortex
Brain
Left visual cortex
Optic nerve
Left eye

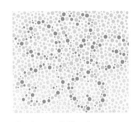

Colour blindness

If you can't see a picture here, you may be colour blind. Colour blindness affects about one in 12 boys or men. It is less common in girls and women.

How do you see colour?

There are six-and-a-half million cone cells in the retina which respond to either red, green or blue light. Light reaching the retina stimulates different combinations of the three types of cones to produce all the colours that we can see. If one type of cone cell is missing, or faulty, then you cannot see a particular colour or combination of colours. This is known as colour blindness.

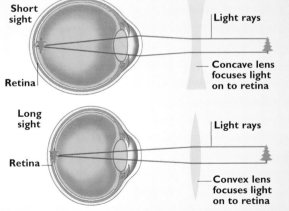

Looking at a picture

The orange area in this PET scan (see p.78) shows the area that is activated at the back of the brain when you look at a picture.

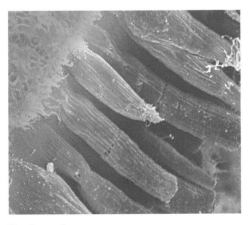

Rods and cones

Cells in the retina are either rods or cones. Cones work in bright light and provide colour and detail. Rods react to light but cannot pick out colours. They are useful for seeing in dim light. There are many more rods than cones.

HELPING AND HEALING

Correcting vision

Muscles change the shape of the lens so that your eye can focus light from objects at different distances away. Sometimes the lens cannot focus the image, usually because the eyeball is too long, or too short so what you see is blurred. Glasses or contact lenses work by bending the light rays so that a clear image reaches your retina.

Short sight
Retina
Light rays
Concave lens focuses light on to retina

Long sight
Retina
Light rays
Convex lens focuses light on to retina

Short and long sight

In short sight, rays from distant objects are focused in front of the retina, so only objects near to you are seen clearly. In long sight, rays from close objects are focused behind the retina, so only distant objects are seen clearly. Special lenses can correct both conditions.

Hearing

All sound begins with vibrations in the air that are like ripples in a pond. As the vibrations reach your ear, they pass through your eardrum, which is about the size of your little finger nail, to several tiny bones in the middle ear. When these bones move, they send impulses to a special nerve (the cochlear nerve). This connects directly with your brain, which makes sense of the signals. Your ears also help you to balance, so that you can stand or walk without toppling over. This is because the inner ear is sensitive to tiny head movements and passes information about space, motion and gravity to the brain (see right).

What is inside your ear?

There are three parts to your ear – the outer, middle and inner ear. The outer ear is the bit you can see on the side of your head. It leads to a narrow passage, about 2 cm long, called the auditory canal. At the end of this is the eardrum. The middle ear is on the other side of the eardrum and is an air-filled hole inside the skull. It is connected to the back of your nose, which is why your ear may be affected when you have a cold. The middle ear also connects with the inner ear, set deeper in the skull. The inner ear is filled with fluid and transfers sound signals directly to the brain.

External ear

Outer ear

Your outer ear is made of cartilage covered in skin. It funnels sound into your auditory canal to reach your eardrum. This canal is lined with thin skin, which produces wax. The wax cleans and moistens the canal, and is gradually wafted towards the outside world by tiny hairs.

Sound wave passing through your ear

Auditory canal (outer

Hairs

Ear examination
With a torch and a magnifying instrument called an auroscope, your doctor can see whether your auditory canal and eardrum appear healthy.

KEEPING HEALTHY

Too loud!
Sound is measured in decibels. Normal speech is about 60 decibels. A loud rock concert might be about 100 decibels. Any sound over 120 decibels can cause pain. More than 140 decibels can damage the delicate hair cells in your inner ear if you listen to it for a long time.

Middle ear

Your middle ear contains the three delicate ossicle bones: the malleus, shaped like a mallet; the incus, shaped like an anvil; and the stapes, shaped like a stirrup. They are connected to each other so that vibrations produced by the sound waves travel from one bone to the next. The middle ear is connected to the back of the nose by the Eustachian tube.

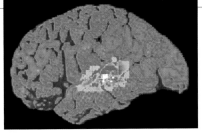

Listening

This PET scan (see p.78) shows the part of the brain that is activated when you listen to sound.

Balance

The inner ear contains three fluid-filled tubes (semicircular canals) set at right angles to each other. When you move your head, fluid inside the canals shifts. The hair cells lining the canals sense the movement and send new information about the position of your head to your brain. The brain can then adjust your posture by sending signals to your muscles.

Inner ear

The bones in your ear join up with a tube that is wound up like a snail's shell. The tube, or cochlea, is filled with fluid and lined by small hairs. The hair cells move slightly when vibrations reach it and this generates electrical signals which are sent along the auditory nerve to the brain.

Perfect balance

This ballet dancer has a well-developed sense of balance learned from years of practice.

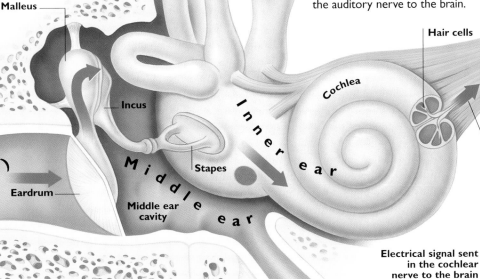

Semicircular canals

Malleus

Incus

Eardrum

Stapes

Middle ear cavity

Middle ear

Inner ear

Cochlea

Hair cells

Electrical signal sent in the cochlear nerve to the brain

Temporal bone of the skull

Eustachian tube

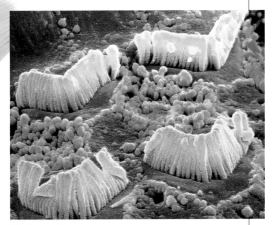

Hair cells

This is a magnified image of the hair cells inside the semicircular canals. When your head moves, hairs like these tilt, sending messages to the brain about the position of your head.

DID YOU KNOW?

Sound direction

Having two ears helps you decide where a sound is coming from. Sound arrives at one ear before the other which enables you to turn towards that side to hear better.

Light and sound

When a firework goes off, you can see the light before you hear the sound. This is because light travels faster than sound.

Mini bones

The malleus, incus and stapes in your middle ear are the smallest bones in your body.

HELPING AND HEALING

Aids to hearing

Most deaf people can hear some sounds, and these can be amplified with a hearing aid. Aids are either moulded to fit inside the ear, or worn behind the ear and connected to a small tube that fits inside the ear canal.

Electronic aids

A cochlear implant is an electronic device, put in under a general anaesthetic, that partially restores hearing to someone who is totally deaf. After receiving an implant, a person can hear some sounds but will not have normal hearing. Combined with lip-reading, the implant should make it easier for a deaf person to understand speech.

Cochlear implant

A microphone behind the ear connects to a transmitter that signals to the cochlear nerve.

Taste and Smell

Eating and drinking would be very boring without your senses of smell and taste, but these senses do not just provide pleasure at mealtimes. They also protect you from eating anything that might be poisonous and from breathing in harmful fumes.

What is your tongue for?

Your tongue is a muscle that can move in many directions to help you to eat, swallow and speak. You also use your tongue to clean your lips and teeth. Its surface is rough because it is covered in little bumps (papillae) containing taste buds. Underneath your tongue is a piece of tissue called the frenulum that loosely holds it to the floor of your mouth. If your frenulum is very short you may find it hard to stick your tongue out. This condition once gave rise to the expression 'tongue-tied', but it is not harmful in any way.

Surface of the tongue

Papilla

How do you taste and smell things?

Your senses of taste and smell are closely related. All tastes start off as chemicals dissolved in saliva in your mouth. These are detected by taste buds situated on little projections, called papillae, on the tongue. Smells start as chemicals dissolved in mucus in your nose and are detected by smell receptors. Messages are sent along nerves to your brain, which interprets the smells and tastes. This information is often stored with the memory of an experience connected with it. That's why you may find that some smells trigger memories from long ago.

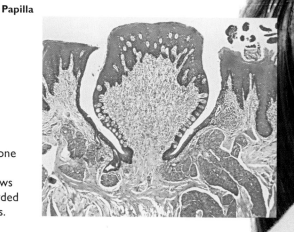

Taste buds
This picture of one papilla under a microscope shows taste buds crowded around the sides.

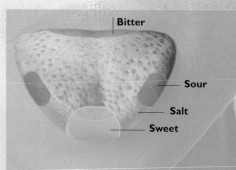

Bitter

Sour

Salt

Sweet

Taste areas

Everything you put in your mouth is a mixture of four tastes: sweet, sour, bitter and salt. Different parts of your tongue detect these tastes: bitter substances are tasted on the back of the tongue, sour along the edges, sweet at the tip and salt just to the sides of sweet. You can detect the four tastes on the roof of your mouth, but there are fewer taste buds there.

TRY IT YOURSELF

Test a friend

Sight is important in recognising food, but you realise how much your sense of smell counts when your nose is blocked up with a cold. Test your sense of taste and smell by taking it in turns to try food while you are blindfolded. To make it more difficult, pinch your nose to stop you from smelling the food as you eat.

Taste and smell test

Cut food such as apple, onion, cheese, potato, strawberry or kiwi fruit, into small cubes, then put them on a cocktail stick. Put on a blindfold and try identifying some of them. Then try to identify the rest while you hold your nose.

Apple

Cube of Cheese

What is your nose for?

If you look at your friends you will see that all noses vary in size and shape. The shape is given by cartilage which makes your nose feel firm. At the lower end of your nose are the two nostrils, separated by a piece of cartilage called the septum. As you breathe in, your nose warms and moistens the air and any dust is trapped in hairs. At the top of your nose is a yellowish area containing smell receptors. This is small in humans compared to other mammals, such as dogs, which have a well-developed sense of smell.

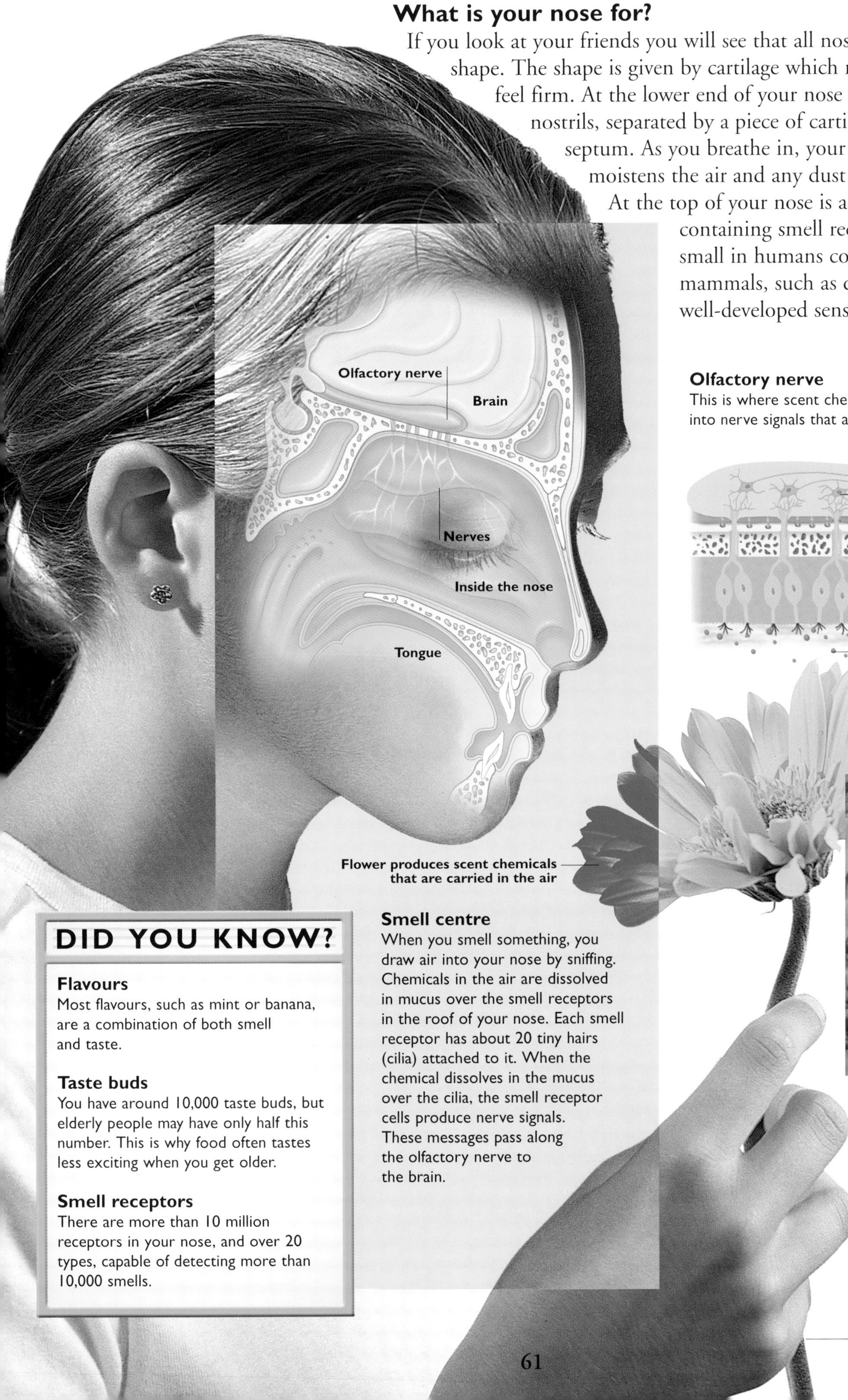

Olfactory nerve
Brain
Nerves
Inside the nose
Tongue

Olfactory nerve
This is where scent chemicals are transformed into nerve signals that are sent to the brain.

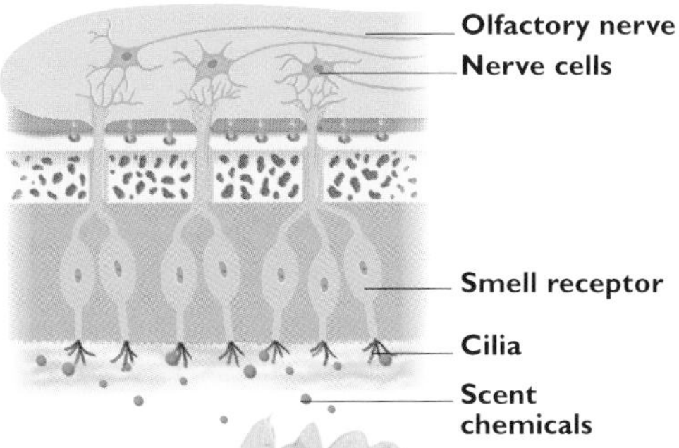

Olfactory nerve
Nerve cells
Smell receptor
Cilia
Scent chemicals

Flower produces scent chemicals that are carried in the air

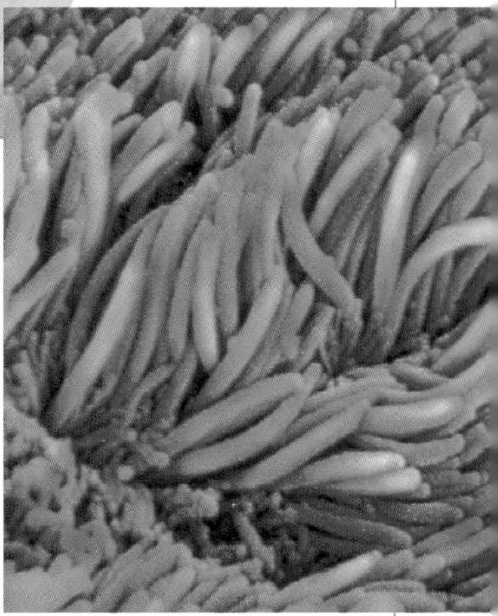

Cilia
This highly magnified picture shows the tiny hair cells, or cilia, that line the surface of the smell receptors in the roof of your nose.

DID YOU KNOW?

Flavours
Most flavours, such as mint or banana, are a combination of both smell and taste.

Taste buds
You have around 10,000 taste buds, but elderly people may have only half this number. This is why food often tastes less exciting when you get older.

Smell receptors
There are more than 10 million receptors in your nose, and over 20 types, capable of detecting more than 10,000 smells.

Smell centre
When you smell something, you draw air into your nose by sniffing. Chemicals in the air are dissolved in mucus over the smell receptors in the roof of your nose. Each smell receptor has about 20 tiny hairs (cilia) attached to it. When the chemical dissolves in the mucus over the cilia, the smell receptor cells produce nerve signals. These messages pass along the olfactory nerve to the brain.

The Cycle of Life

EVERY LIFE STARTS WITH FERTILIZATION
of an egg cell by a sperm. Thereafter the physical
development of a person, from embryo
to baby, child, and adult occurs by a
process of continual cell growth and
division. The whole life cycle is
influenced and controlled by the
genes inside your cells.

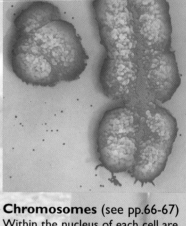

Chromosomes (see pp.66-67)
Within the nucleus of each cell are
structures called chromosomes (two
are shown above). Chromosomes
contain units called genes that
control how your body cells work.

Cells (see pp.64-65)
Your body's building blocks are
billions of cells. There are many types
of cells, such as muscle cells (shown
above), nerve cells, and so on.
Different types of cells have different
shapes and functions, but nearly every
cell has a control region at its centre
called a nucleus.

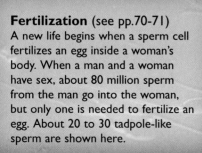

Fertilization (see pp.70-71)
A new life begins when a sperm cell
fertilizes an egg inside a woman's
body. When a man and a woman
have sex, about 80 million sperm
from the man go into the woman,
but only one is needed to fertilize an
egg. About 20 to 30 tadpole-like
sperm are shown here.

DNA
(see pp.68-69)
Your genes are made from a substance called DNA. Every person's DNA is unique – a person's identity can be proved from his or her DNA pattern.

Adulthood
When a person reaches adulthood, he or she is usually capable of continuing the cycle of life by having children, though some choose not to. As adults grow older, signs of ageing become obvious. A healthy lifestyle helps people stay fit well into old age.

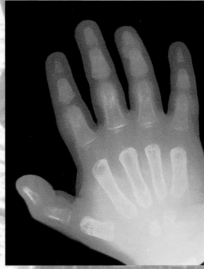

Growing up
(see pp.74-75)
Huge changes occur in the first 10 years. From a dependent baby, you learn to walk, talk, feed and dress yourself, read and write. As a baby, your bones were mainly cartilage (shown as pink), but this is gradually replaced by bone (shown as yellow).

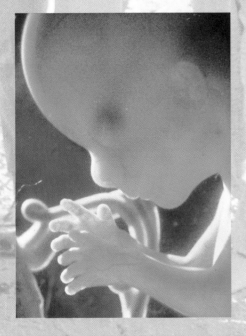

Developing fetus
(see pp.72-73)
It takes nine months for a fertilized egg cell to grow into a fully formed baby, ready to be born. This picture shows the fetus's face and arms at 16 weeks.

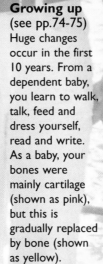

Cells

The skin on your body may appear smooth, but if you look at your hand with a magnifying glass, it looks a bit like crazy paving with tiny hairs sticking out. Each piece of 'paving' is a group of skin cells. With a very powerful microscope, you could look at each part of your body and see that it's made of millions of tiny individual cells. There are many types of cell, each with different jobs to do. Groups of similar cells join together to make tissues, which form organs, such as the liver (see right).

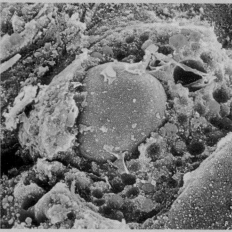

Adrenal gland cell
This image shows a single cell in an adrenal gland. The brown region is the cell nucleus. The orange blobs are droplets of fat.

What are cells?

A body is made of cells in the same way that a house can be built out of thousands of bricks. Each cell in your body is much smaller than the sharp end of a pin, so it is invisible to the naked eye. Every person starts life as a single egg cell, which is fertilized by a sperm cell. This fertilized egg cell divides into two identical cells. Each of these divides, and so four cells are produced. The cell division continues until a cluster of many hundreds of cells, called an embryo, develops. Gradually, individual cells in the embryo start to change shape, according to their special functions: some become nerve cells, some muscle cells and so on. However, every cell has a control region, called a nucleus, at its centre, surrounded by a jelly-like substance called cytoplasm. Red blood cells are the only cells without a nucleus.

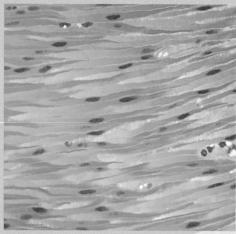

Muscle cells
These elongated cells can change their length as special interlocking filaments in their cytoplasm slide past each other.

HELPING AND HEALING

Cell regeneration

Some tissues (collections of cells) can regenerate when they are damaged, through the remaining healthy cells dividing to make new ones. For example, if you graze the skin on your knee, it will form a scab. When the scab falls off, there will be new skin underneath. If you have a more serious injury, such as a severe burn, when the entire outer layer of your skin has been destroyed, the cells may be unable to regrow. In this case, you need a skin graft: a thin layer of skin taken from another part of your body is used to cover the damaged area.

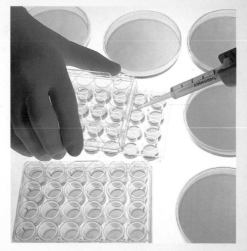

Cell cultures
Some cells, including skin cells, can be made to divide and grow in a laboratory, given the right nutrients. This is called 'culturing' cells.

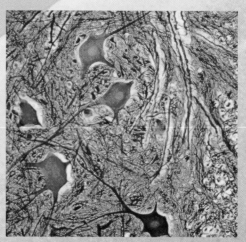

Nerve cells
These cells (seen here as brown blobs) have numerous projections, along which electrical messages can be passed to and from other nerve cells, or to muscle cells.

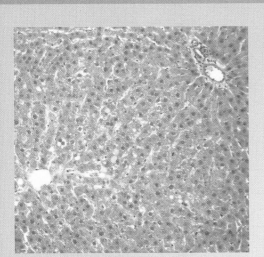

Liver cells
Liver cells are arranged in layers surrounded by blood to allow nutrients and toxic material to flow easily from one to another.

Hair cells
Some cells lining the airways have tiny surface hairs like these. The hairs waft dust and germs out of the lungs and back up to the throat.

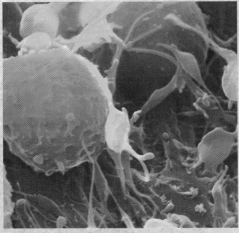

Blood cells
Blood contains three types of cells. Red cells carry oxygen, white cells fight infection and platelets (seen here as small yellow blobs) help blood to clot after injury.

A typical human cell
At the centre of a cell is the nucleus, which controls the cell. Outside the nucleus is the cytoplasm, which contains many tiny structures. These are involved in producing energy for the cell, destroying worn-out parts, and making new chemicals that the body needs. Surrounding the whole cell is a covering called the cell membrane.

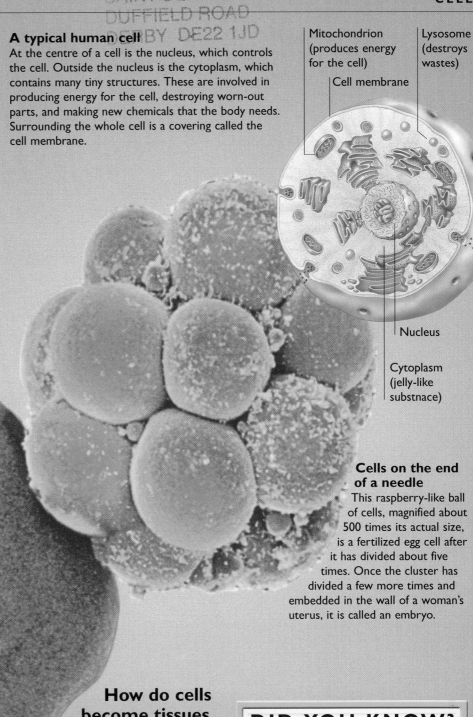

Mitochondrion (produces energy for the cell)

Lysosome (destroys wastes)

Cell membrane

Nucleus

Cytoplasm (jelly-like substnace)

Cells on the end of a needle
This raspberry-like ball of cells, magnified about 500 times its actual size, is a fertilized egg cell after it has divided about five times. Once the cluster has divided a few more times and embedded in the wall of a woman's uterus, it is called an embryo.

How do cells become tissues and organs?
A tissue is a collection of many similar cells in one place, for example, a group of muscle cells together form muscle tissue. An organ is a group of tissues that work together to perform a particular task. For example, the heart is an organ that contains muscle, some fibrous tissue, and some nerve tissue. Different tissues arise from identical cells during the development of an embryo.

DID YOU KNOW?

Minuscule cells
There are around 10 billion cells in your body. Around 40 of them would fit on a full stop.

Same-size cells
The cells of a whale or a fly are the same size as those of a human. The whale is bigger because it has more cells, not because the cells are larger.

Mega-cells
Some of your nerve cells have projections (called axons) 30 cm long or more, running from your spinal cord to your hands and feet.

Chromosomes and Genes

Each cell in your body contains a set of instructions, called 'genes', that control the activities of that cell. You received some of these genes from your mother and some from your father. Altogether there are about 150,000 genes in each cell. To fit them in, they are strung together in long chains that are coiled up in structures called chromosomes.

What are chromosomes?

Chromosomes are tiny rod-shaped structures in the nuclei of cells. There are 23 pairs of them, making 46 chromosomes in all. Sperm and egg cells only have a single set of 23 chromosomes. When an egg and sperm combine, they have the full complement of chromosomes.

What are genes?

A gene is a section of a chromosome that codes for the production of a substance known as a protein. This protein is used within that cell, or is exported for use in another part of the body. Although every cell in your body (except for egg and sperm cells) contains a full set of genes, not every cell uses every single gene: many of these genes are 'switched off'. The study of genes is called genetics.

Chromosomes

Nuclear membrane

Nucleus

Chromosomes

Cell nucleus
The nucleus of the cell contains the genes, held in chromosomes.

Appearance of chromosomes
A chromosome is normally shaped like a rod. Before a cell divides, each chromosome copies itself into two rods, joined at their centres in the shape of an X. All the chromosomes on this page are 'doubled-up' in this way. When the cell divides, the two copies of each chromosome part company and go into the two new cells.

Super coiled structure
If viewed very close up, a chromosome can be seen to be arranged in a tight coil.

DNA

Karyotype
If a person's chromosomes are photographed under a microscope, and images of the individual chromosomes are then cut up and arranged by size, as here, you can see that there are 23 pairs. This procedure is called 'karyotyping'.

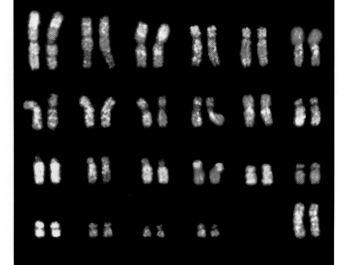

HELPING AND HEALING

Amniocentesis

During pregnancy, a sample of the fluid surrounding the baby can be obtained via a needle inserted into the mother's womb. The fluid contains some of the baby's cells, whose chromosomes can be inspected. This test, called amniocentesis, can reveal the baby's sex and any problems with the chromosomes.

How do you inherit genes?

Your genes determine how your body works, how you look, and what diseases you are prone to. Many genes are the same from one person to the next, but others differ, and it is the particular 'mix' of genes you possess that makes you different from everyone else. A parent passes on half of his or her genes to each child – so, half of your genes come from your mother and half from your father. The way in which genes are passed from parents to children, and how genes from the father and mother interact in the child, is called 'genetic inheritance'.

Family resemblances
Closely-related members of families share a high proportion of their genes. As a result, individual members often look like each other. They may also be prone to the same diseases.

X chromosome

Y chromosome

X and Y chromosomes
Each cell has two sex chromosomes, one inherited from each parent. Everybody receives a sex chromosome called an X chromosome from his or her mother. A girl inherits another X chromosome from her father, so she has two X chromosomes. However, a boy receives a different, much smaller chromosome from his father, called the Y chromosome.

DNA structure
If deoxyribonucleic acid (DNA) is looked at through a powerful microscope, it can be seen to have a complex 'double helix' structure, like a twisted ladder (see p.68).

DNA double helix

TRY IT YOURSELF

The bead game
To mimic how sex is determined, suppose red beads represent 'X' chromosomes and blue beads, 'Y' chromosomes. Put 20 red beads in one container (the 'mother') and a mix of 10 red and 10 blue beads in another (the 'father'). Close your eyes and pick a bead from each container. Two reds make a girl, a red and a blue, a boy.

Rolling your tongue
Can you make your tongue look like this? Not everyone can – how many of your friends can do it? The ability to do this is inherited. If you can roll your tongue, at least one of your parents should be able to do so, too.

Analysing the Blueprint

Fingerprints
Until now only your fingerprints identified you as an individual. Now we know that the structure of your DNA can give further proof of your identity.

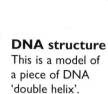

DNA structure
This is a model of a piece of DNA 'double helix'.

In the days before computers, architects and engineers used a written plan or drawing of the work to be done, which was known as a blueprint. Each of us has a unique set of instructions about how each cell in our body should behave. This human blueprint is situated in the nucleus of every cell.

What is DNA ?

On the previous page, you read about your chromosomes and genes. There are 46 chromosomes in each of a person's cells, except egg and sperm cells, which have only 23 chromosomes. These chromosomes contain a long thread-like substance called DNA (deoxyribonucleic acid).

DNA has a complicated structure that resembles a twisted ladder. The two sides of the ladder each contain a type of sugar and a substance, called phosphate, linked together in a long chain. In the middle of the DNA molecule, forming the rungs of the ladder, are chemicals called nucleotide bases. The bases on each strand pair off together, linking the two sugar-phosphate side-chains. There are four kinds of base, but each one will only pair with one of the other three.

The overall structure of DNA, with the two side-chains twisting continuously around each other, is often called a 'double helix.'

The DNA double helix
In this partly untwisted piece of DNA, pairs of bases can be seen linking the two side-chains. There are four kinds of base: thymine, adenine, guanine, and cytosine. Thymine and adenine always pair off together, as do guanine and cytosine. A gene consists of a section of DNA, hundreds of base-pairs in length. The order of the bases carries a gene's instructions in coded form.

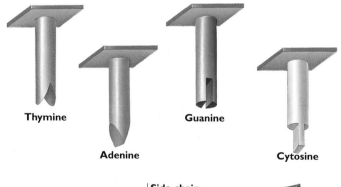

Thymine

Adenine

Guanine

Cytosine

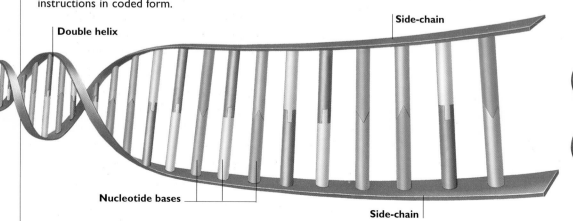

Double helix

Side-chain

Nucleotide bases

Side-chain

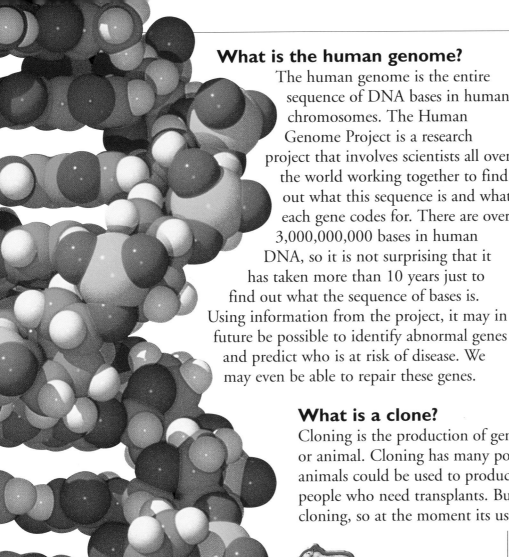

What is the human genome?

The human genome is the entire sequence of DNA bases in human chromosomes. The Human Genome Project is a research project that involves scientists all over the world working together to find out what this sequence is and what each gene codes for. There are over 3,000,000,000 bases in human DNA, so it is not surprising that it has taken more than 10 years just to find out what the sequence of bases is. Using information from the project, it may in future be possible to identify abnormal genes and predict who is at risk of disease. We may even be able to repair these genes.

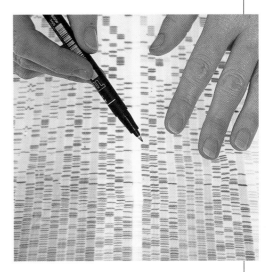

DNA fingerprinting
The sequence of DNA in a sample of hair or body fluid, such as saliva or blood, can identify a person and has been used by police to help solve some serious crimes.

What is a clone?

Cloning is the production of genetically identical copies of a plant or animal. Cloning has many potential uses. For example, cloned animals could be used to produce certain medicines, or organs, for people who need transplants. But people have some worries about cloning, so at the moment its use is restricted.

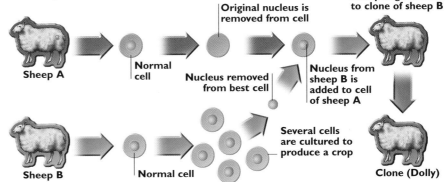

Sheep A → Normal cell → Original nucleus is removed from cell → Nucleus from sheep B is added to cell of sheep A → Sheep A gives birth to clone of sheep B

Nucleus removed from best cell

Sheep B → Normal cell → Several cells are cultured to produce a crop → Clone (Dolly)

Dolly the sheep
In 1998, a sheep called Dolly was born. To produce Dolly researchers took a single cell from the udder of a sheep. They removed the nucleus, which contained a full set of sheep's chromosomes, and using tiny needles, placed it into a sheep egg cell. (The nucleus of the egg had already been removed.) Normally the udder cell would be able to produce milk only. But when the udder cell nucleus was implanted into the egg cell, it developed into an embryo, and finally became Dolly.

HELPING AND HEALING

Gene therapy

Many diseases, such as cystic fibrosis and sickle cell disease, are inherited. The Human Genome Project has located the genes that cause many of these conditions, making it possible to consider replacing the affected gene with a normal gene and so cure the disease. This is known as gene therapy, and it is still in its early stages. So far, it has been possible to alleviate genetic disease in a few sufferers by replacing the affected gene in some of the person's cells. One day, it may be possible to alter an affected gene so that it is not passed on to a person's children, but at present there are obstacles to achieving this.

Reproduction and Fertilization

Most women have the potential to produce a new human being. Every month, a woman's body releases a tiny egg cell from one of her ovaries. On its own, this egg cannot become a baby. It has to be joined by a sperm cell from a man, in a process known as fertilization. From this fertilized egg, a baby can develop.

A woman's body produces hormones from the pituitary gland (see p.38), which make her body produce an egg every month. It also makes her ovaries produce hormones called oestrogen and progesterone that help to prepare her body if the egg is fertilized.

The female and male reproductive organs

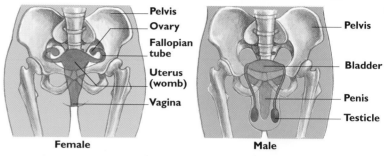

Female

Male

Where are your reproductive organs?

A boy's reproductive organs are his testicles and penis. The testicles are in a bag of skin called the scrotum. Sperm develops inside the testicles. To develop normally, sperm needs to be kept cool, which is why the scrotum hangs outside a boy's body between his legs.

The testicles are connected to the penis by tubes. During sex, about a teaspoon of creamy fluid containing 80 million sperm leaves the man's body via the penis, and goes into the woman's vagina.

A girl's reproductive organs include her ovaries, uterus (womb) and fallopian tubes. The ovaries hold about 150,000 eggs that are released one at a time, once a month, into the fallopian tube.

The uterus is the size of an apricot, but it can stretch to allow a baby to grow inside it. The vagina is a muscular tube, open to the outside at one end, and connecting via the cervix to the uterus at the other end. During childbirth, the cervix opens and the vagina stretches to allow the baby to travel through.

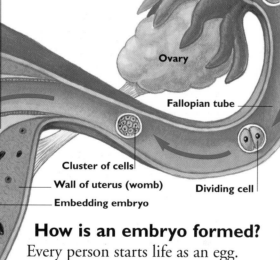

How is an embryo formed?

Every person starts life as an egg. This egg leaves the ovary on an amazing journey. Somewhere in the fallopian tube, the egg is joined (fertilized) by a sperm, one of millions from the father that travel up the vagina, through the uterus (womb) and into the fallopian tube. This fertilized egg divides into two cells, and then these two cells divide into four cells, and these four cells divided into eight cells, and so on. This rapidly dividing bundle of cells buries itself deep in the mother's uterus and forms a growing embryo.

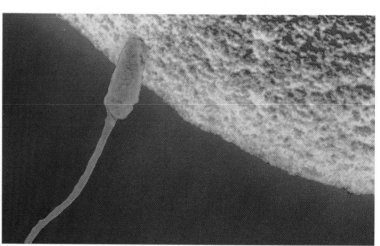

1. Fertilizing the egg
Of around 80 million sperm that go into the woman's body during sex, only one is needed to fertilize the egg. In this picture you can see a sperm cell penetrating the outer surface of the egg.

How do twins grow?
Identical twins are formed when a single fertilized egg divides to produce two embryos.

5. An embryo 4 weeks after fertilization
The fertilized cells continue to divide rapidly, and then different groups of cells start to develop into the different organs.

4. Implantation
At around 4-7 days after fertilization, the ball of cells buries itself into the lining of the prepared uterus.

3. Fast division
The fertilized egg continues to divide rapidly as it travels along the fallopian tube, forming a ball of cells.

What happens if an egg is not fertilized?
Each month, when an egg is released, the hormones produced by the ovaries make the lining of the uterus get thicker and spongier, so that it is ready for a fertilized egg. The egg can only survive for 24 hours after it has been released. If it is not fertilized, it leaves the woman's body via the vagina, together with the lining of the uterus and about half a cup of blood. This happens once a month, and is known as menstruation. Most women have their menstruation, or 'period', about every 28 days, and it usually lasts for around three to five days.

Two cells

2. Two cells
In the first few hours after fertilization, the egg divides into two.

HELPING AND HEALING

Assisted fertilization
As many as one in ten couples have problems producing a baby. Scientists are able help these couples with a technique called in-vitro fertilization, or IVF. This involves mixing the sperm and egg cells outside the woman's body in a test tube. Once it has been fertilized, using the IVF technique, the egg is put back into the mother's uterus. Successful pregnancies occur in around 15% of cases. If more than one egg is put in at a time, twins, triplets, quads or even more babies can result.

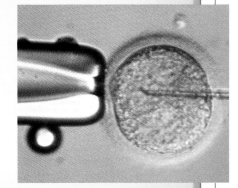

IVF technique
While the egg (above) is held steady, a sperm is injected into it.

The Developing Baby

Pregnancy begins when a fertilized egg implants in the womb. The womb lining doesn't shed and so a woman's monthly periods stop. This is the first sign of pregnancy. She may feel a bit tired and, perhaps, nauseous, and her breasts may feel tender. For several months, the woman's shape doesn't change much, because the developing baby is very small. But vast changes are happening inside her body. In less than a year, a new person develops inside her womb.

How does an unborn baby develop?

At first the embryo is a ball of cells that buries itself in the wall of the womb. Within a week, the cells have changed, each of them designed to become a particular part of the baby's body. By 8 weeks, the embryo is recognisable as a human being, and is known as a fetus. It is still only 3 cm long. Between 8 and 12 weeks, it grows rapidly, increasing its weight by up to 15 times. By the time the baby is born, it weighs, on average, about 3 kg.

HELPING AND HEALING

What the baby needs

The mother's diet is very important for the health of the developing fetus. If she eats a balanced, healthy diet, it helps to ensure that the fetus grows normally. It also reduces the baby's risk of ill health in later life. Medicines taken by the mother may reach the circulation of the fetus, where they may be harmful. So pregnant women need to be cautious about taking tablets without first checking with a doctor. Pregnant women are also advised to avoid alcohol and cigarettes, which can limit the normal development of the fetus.

How long does a pregnancy last?

The developing embryo buries itself in the wall of the womb one week after it is fertilized. About 9 months, or 40 weeks, after the mother's last period, the baby will be fully formed. Sometimes the baby is born early. If it is more than 3 weeks early, it is described as a premature baby, because it may not be fully developed. About 2% of babies are born 6 weeks early. Babies born as much as 17 weeks early have a good chance of surviving, thanks to recent advances in the care of premature babies in specialised intensive care units.

How a baby develops

8 weeks
The fetus is the size of a jelly bean. Although the womb is getting bigger, the pregnant woman may not look very different at this early stage.

24 weeks
Gradually her tummy grows as the baby inside the womb gets bigger. You may even be able to feel the baby kicking if you rest your hand on her tummy.

40 weeks
The baby is fully grown. Other organs in the woman's tummy may be squashed aside, and she may feel uncomfortable.

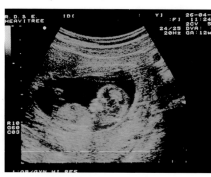

Ultrasound scan

The ultrasound machine detects and records echoes from high frequency sound waves and converts them into a grainy picture which shows the growing baby. From information about its size, doctors can work out the baby's age in weeks.

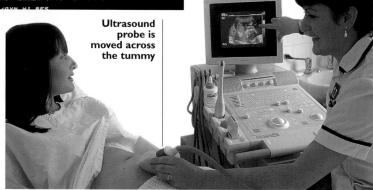

Ultrasound probe is moved across the tummy

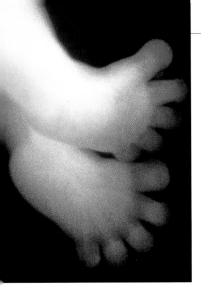

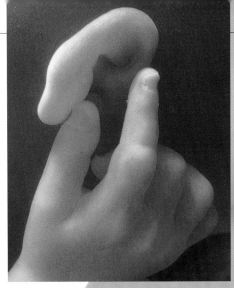

DID YOU KNOW?

Inside the womb
• By 10 weeks, the fetus' nervous system has developed enough for it to be capable of feeling pain.
• The baby can hear noises from outside the womb.
• Most babies come out head first. Only around 3% are born bottom first, and are known as breech babies.
• Did you know that the fetus may get hiccups while still inside its mother?

Feet
The feet begin to develop at 7 weeks and by 11 weeks, toenails have started to form. By the time the fetus is 36 weeks old, the toenails are fully grown.

Ears and hands
The hand starts to form at 6 weeks and is fully formed at 32 weeks. Here, the fetus is shown feeling its ear at 20 weeks.

How does an unborn baby eat or breathe?
The growing fetus cannot eat or breathe until it is born. It is completely dependent on its mother for nourishment and oxygen. Blood flows from the mother into the placenta, a spongy mound of tissue attached to the inside of the womb. The fetus is joined to the placenta by the umbilical cord. Oxygen and nutrients drift from the mother's blood into the placenta, and are taken to the fetus via the umbilical cord. The placenta also gets blood from the fetus through the umbilical cord. This blood contains carbon dioxide and waste chemicals, which filter into the mother's blood in the placenta. She gets rid of these wastes in her lungs (see p.30) and kidneys (see p.36). Your navel is where the umbilical cord once attached you to your mother's body.

Baby
The fetus is surrounded by a protective, fluid-filled bag known as the amniotic sac. This fluid is mainly water. It is made by the amniotic sac, swallowed by the fetus and passed out into the amniotic fluid via the baby's kidneys. By the 35th week, there is about 1 litre of fluid, but this falls to about 500 ml by 40 weeks. By the end of pregnancy, the baby doesn't have much room to move, and is tightly curled up inside the uterus.

Development of the face
The face develops over several weeks. At first, the eyes are on either side of the head and the nose is flat with widely-spaced nostrils. Gradually the features move and, by 16 weeks, they are in position. At this point they start to look more like a baby's face.

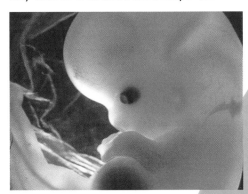

Development at 7 weeks

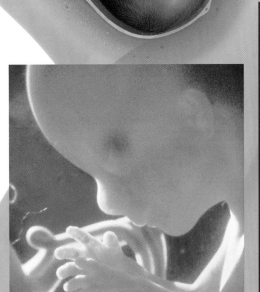

Development at 16 weeks

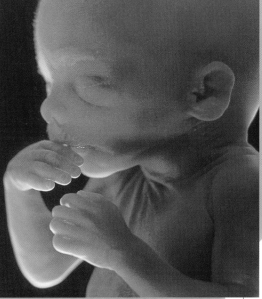

Development at 20 weeks

Growing up

When you were born, there was little that you could do for yourself. If you wanted to be fed, turned over, or have your nappy changed, you had to cry until the person looking after you understood. Gradually, as your muscles and bones developed, you learned how to move yourself from one place to another and how to communicate. Most babies learn things like walking and talking at specific times, but there is a big range in what is regarded as normal.

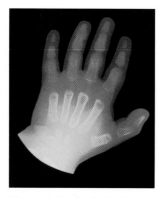

X-ray of a baby's hand
A newborn baby has only a small amount of bone in its skeleton. The rest is cartilage.

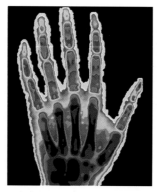

An 8-year-old's hand
Over time, bone (blue, black, and green areas in this X-ray) replaces the cartilage.

KEEPING HEALTHY

Safety first
A growing child loves to explore and has to be kept safe by others until it understands the dangers of its environment. This means ensuring that objects that could be swallowed, or cause injury to the child, are kept out of reach, or locked in a cupboard.

Windows should also be kept locked so that a child cannot crawl out.

Water safety
All children should be supervised when playing near to or in water.

Physical skills
A newborn baby makes random, or reflex movements with his arms and legs, but can't hold his head up without support. Gradually, he learns to control the movements he makes. First he holds his own head up, next he learns to roll over, then sit, crawl stand and walk.

Lifting head
By three months old, a baby placed on his tummy can lift his head and hold it up to look around.

Hand-eye co-ordination
A newborn baby can see, but unless the object is held close to her eyes, it appears blurred. By six months a baby can see across a room. As her vision improves, she learns to control the muscles of each hand so that she can handle small objects, such as a switch or a screw.

Reaching
A baby aged three to five months can reach out for a rattle held towards her, or grab at objects hanging over her.

Hearing and language
A newborn baby is startled by loud noises, an early sign that he can hear. With time, the baby learns to understand and recognise sounds. At first, a baby can only make himself understood by crying. But very soon a baby learns to control the sounds he makes, and gradually the sounds become recognisable words.

Behaviour and play
Every baby has to learn about other people. As a child grows up, it learns how to play with other children and how to make friends. Sharing, taking turns, exchanging news are all 'social skills'. A child also has to learn how to look after itself and become independent.

Early play
A baby's first games centre on her parents. At six months, she can play peekaboo and, by a year old, she will copy an adult doing the housework. By 18 months, a toddler may enjoy a playgroup, and will gradually learn to play with other children.

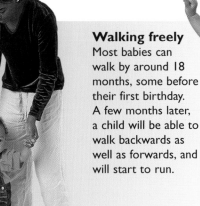
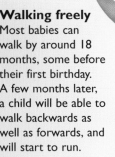

Crawling

At around six months, some babies start trying to crawl, and most can crawl by about nine months. Some crawl backwards before they crawl forwards, some learn to walk without crawling, others move about by shuffling along on their bottoms, rather than crawling.

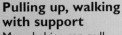

Pulling up, walking with support

Many babies can pull themselves up to stand from 6 to 10 months. From 10 to 14 months, babies may walk around a room holding onto the furniture, or holding onto an adult for support.

Walking freely

Most babies can walk by around 18 months, some before their first birthday. A few months later, a child will be able to walk backwards as well as forwards, and will start to run.

Stacking

At about one year, a child can pick up a small object between the thumb and index finger. At around 15 to 18 months, a child is beginning to be able to build with bricks. By the age of two years, most children can build a tower of four bricks.

Threading

At the age of three years, a child can thread a piece of string through a marble-sized hole in a plastic disc.

Painting/writing

At 18 months, most children enjoy scribbling with a crayon. By four years of age, the drawings are recognisable: a picture of a person will probably have a face and maybe arms and legs.

Learning to talk

At eight months, a baby can be tested for hearing because by this age he should turn his head towards the source of a sound. He will already be making attempts at copying sound patterns. A baby makes cooing sounds from around three months old and by about six months, he is 'babbling', saying sounds like 'dada' and 'mama', although he doesn't know what they mean. Between nine and 12 months, the baby will realise that his parents respond to 'mama and 'dada'.

Most babies have spoken their first words by the time they are one year old, and by the age of two they can put two words together. At three years old, many children can name colours and talk in simple but full sentences, as well as chant rhymes.

A child who is learning more than one language may take longer than other children to start talking.

Socialising

As a child grows up, friendships can become more complicated. But spending time with friends is always a good way to share experiences.

From Child to Adult

By the time you are in your early twenties, your body will have reached physical maturity. This is the time when your body is at its strongest. Girls start to develop their adult bodies earlier than boys, on average. Most people do not become emotionally mature for some years after their body appears to have matured.

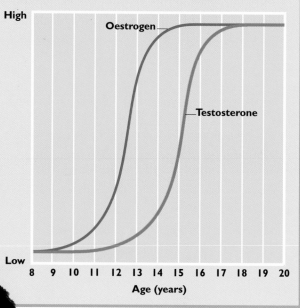

What is puberty?

There is a period of transition between childhood and adulthood known as adolescence. During this time, your body changes and begins to look more like an adult. The changes that take place are known as puberty. This is a period of rapid growth, and many chemical changes occur inside your body. You may need more sleep and food to meet your body's new demands for energy.

Puberty starts when a small gland in your brain known as the pituitary gland starts to produce hormones that stimulate the ovaries in girls and testes in boys. The ovaries start producing progesterone and oestrogen, and the testes start producing testosterone.

The rise in oestrogen (girls) and testosterone (boys) at puberty

High

Oestrogen

Testosterone

Low

| 8 | 9 | 10 | 11 | 12 | 13 | 14 | 15 | 16 | 17 | 18 | 19 | 20 |

Age (years)

Rise of the hormones

At puberty there is a rapid rise in hormone production. This starts earlier in girls (around the age of 10 or 11) than in boys (12 to 13). It levels off at around age 15 in girls and 18 in boys.

Making new friends
Both girls and boys become much more interested in sex and relationships during adolescence. Along with other changes, this is caused by the rise in hormone production in both sexes.

KEEPING HEALTHY

Adolescence

Most adolescents experiment with their image. You may be very self-conscious about your appearance and sensitive to criticism. It can be particularly difficult to maintain your confidence if you have spots. Acne is caused by hormonal changes, not by how much chocolate or greasy food you eat. However, it is treatable, so consult your doctor for advice.

Puberty is often accompanied by huge emotional changes. Relationships with parents can become strained at this time. Try to carry on talking to them, choosing topics that are not going to cause an argument. You may need to fall back on your family for support later on. Many adolescents experience pressure from friends or acquaintances. Sometimes this can lead them to try something that they are not ready for, like sex. Before you do anything, be sure it is right for you.

What happens to a girl's body?

As puberty progresses, a girl will notice a spurt in her growth. As she grows taller, her breasts gradually start to enlarge and she starts growing hair in the pubic region and under her arms. Her hips broaden but her shoulders stay narrow. All these changes are due to the effects of the hormones oestrogen and progesterone.

What are periods?

About a year after puberty starts, a girl starts ovulating – which means an egg is released every month from one of her ovaries. The lining of the womb thickens, ready to receive a fertilized egg. If the egg is not fertilized by a sperm, the womb lining is shed, together with the egg, causing bleeding for a few days from the vagina. This is what is known as a period. When periods first start, they may be irregular.

What happens to a boy's body?

Boys also experience a growth spurt. The rise in testosterone causes new hair to grow in the same regions as in girls, but also on his chest and face. A boy's shoulders broaden, his muscles grow bigger and stronger, and his voice becomes deeper. His penis and testes enlarge. By the time a boy is 15, his testes can make 200 million new sperm every day.

What happens as you get older?

As you get older, the number of cells in your body gradually falls, partly because cells die and are not replaced, and the ones that are left tend to malfunction more often. However, the effects of cell loss and malfunctioning are not felt by most people until they are well past the age of 40, or even older. It is possible to do most things in life until well into old age.

DID YOU KNOW?

Life expectancy
The age to which you can expect to live is partly determined by your genes – if your parents and grandparents live for a long time, you have a good chance of a long life too. You can also increase life expectancy by looking after yourself – through a healthy diet, regular exercise, and by avoiding harmful behaviour such as smoking.

Reproductive limits
Men can continue to have children until they are old, but women stop producing eggs at the menopause, which is at age 50, on average.

Living a full life
As you grow older, your hair turns grey and your skin becomes wrinkled. But you can still enjoy many new interests and friendships.

Guide to Imaging Techniques

Looking inside your body

You may have tried looking at your skin or a hair using a magnifying glass. But have you ever wondered what you look like inside? In the distant past, the only way of finding out was to cut the body open or to take samples of it to examine under a microscope. In the last 100 years, many new imaging techniques have been developed. A selection of the techniques shown elsewhere in this book are explained here.

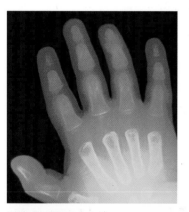

X-ray

An X-ray is a black and white picture of the hard parts inside your body, mainly bone. Bright colours can be added to help make the X-ray clearer. Here you can see that a baby's hand only has a small amount of bone (shown here coloured yellow). The pink parts are cartilage. The blue areas are skin and muscle.

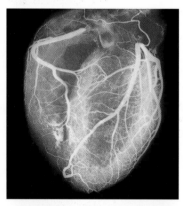

Angiogram

This is a type of X-ray taken after injecting a special dye into one or more blood vessels. The dye appears white on this X-ray and shows up the normal blood vessels supplying the heart (which appears orange-red here). Angiograms are used to detect problems in blood vessels, such as blockages or narrowings.

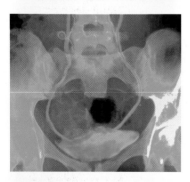

Urogram

Hollow organs like the bladder do not show up well on a plain X-ray. To make this image, a dye was injected into a vein on the back of a person's hand. As the dye left the body in urine, an X-ray was taken. The winding tubes are ureters (urine-carrying ducts). The green area at the bottom is urine pooling in the bladder.

Lung arteriogram

This image is similar to the angiogram of the heart, except here the blood vessels shown (red) are those supplying the lungs (green).

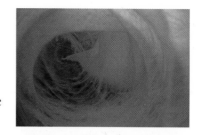

Endoscope

An endoscope is a hollow flexible tube, incorporating a light. The tube's tip is gently pushed through the mouth as far as the stomach or small intestine, shown here. Images can be relayed to a monitor.

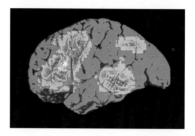

PET scan

A positron emission tomograph (PET) scan is based on detecting how an injected substance is used in an organ such as the brain. This PET scan shows brain areas that are active (yellow) while performing a particular task.

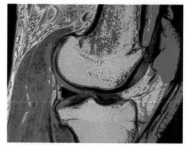

MRI scan

A magnetic resonance image (MRI) is a picture of a slice through the body. It is a painless test using harmless radiation. All the different parts are shown clearly. In this MRI of the knee you can see bone (blue) and muscle (red).

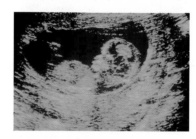

Ultrasound scan

Ultrasound uses inaudible sound waves, which are 'bounced' off internal organs and their reflections detected. Ultrasound is especially useful for examining hollow organs such as the womb, seen here with a fetus inside.

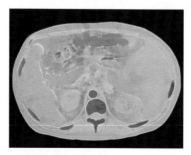

CT scan

CT stands for 'computerized tomography' and is based on taking X-rays of the body from different angles and analyzing the results with a computer. Like MRI, the result is an image of a slice through the body, in this case a slice through the torso.

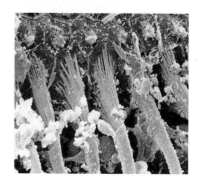

Microscopy

A small piece of tissue removed from the body can be examined using a microscope. There are various strengths of microscope, which can magnify from a few hundreds to many thousands of times. In this picture you can see tiny hair cells (yellow) lining an airway in the lungs.

Index

NOTE: Page numbers in **bold** indicate main sections; those in *italics* indicate illustrations.

List of abbreviations
Metric
cm = centimetres
m = metres
km = kilometres
km/h = kilometres per hour
km² = square kilometres
kg = kilogrammes

Imperial
in = inches
ft = feet
miles = miles
mph = miles per hour
sq miles = square miles
lb = pounds

Acknowledgements
(key: t=top; b=bottom; c=centre; l=left; r=right. SPL=Science Photo Library)
Illustrations
David Ashby 12–13 details, 13tr, 20, 31t, 37, 42, 43bl, 44–45, 48–49, 56b, 57, 61cr; **Peter Bull** 28–29; **Judith Bussmann** 72cr, **Michael Courtney** 17tr, 22, 30cl, 32–33, 43cr, 58–59; **Andrew Farmer** 30cr; **George Fryer** (Bernard Thornton Artists): 18–19, **Kevin Jones Associates** 14–15; **Sean Milne** 8–9, 11bl, 38, 70; **Jon Potter** (Wildlife Art Agency): 73c; **Martin Sanders** 69cr; **Mike Saunders** 10tr; **Guy Smith** 16–17c, 21, 23, 24–25, 30bl, 46–47, 53, 56cr, 65, 66–67, 68; **Leslie D. Smith** 35tr; **Richard Tibbitts** 12–13c, 61c; **Philip Wilson** 7, 40–41.

Photographic Credits
All photography by Adrian Weinbrecht with the exception of the credits listed below. 1 Quest/ SPL; 4tl Quest/ SPL; 5tl Alfred Pasieka/ SPL; 5crt Petit Format/ Nestle/ SPL; 5crb CNRI/ SPL; 5bl Andrew Syred/ SPL; 6l Prof. P. Motta/ Dept. of Anatomy/ University "La Sapienza", Rome/ SPL; 6cb SPL; 6br Richard Wehr/ Custom Medical Stock Photo/ SPL; 7cr Quest/ SPL; 7tr Geoff Tompkinson/ SPL; 7tl BSIP Dr. Pichard T./ SPL; 8cr Richard Wehr/ Custom Medical Stock Photo/ SPL; 8tr Mark Clarke/ SPL; 8cr Richard Wehr/ Custom Medical Stock Photo/ SPL; 9tr Professors P.M. Motta, K.R. Porter & P.M.Andrews/ SPL; 10tc SPL; 10-11 Martin Dohrn/ SPL; 11bc Prof. P. Motta/ Dept. of Anatomy/ University "La Sapienza", Rome/ SPL; 11tr Dept. of Clinical Radiology, Salisbury District Hospital/ SPL; 12bc Dept. of Clinical Radiology, Salisbury District Hospital/ SPL; 13c Geoff Tompkinson/ SPL; 14crt Profs P. M. Motta & E. Vizza/ SPL; 14tr & cr Quest/ SPL; 15br Peter Tarry/ Action-Plus; 16cl BSIP Dr. Pichard T./ SPL; 16tr CNRI/ SPL; 17cr & br CNRI/ SPL; 17tl Mehau Kulyk/ SPL; 18-19 Pictor Uniphoto; 18l NIBSC/ SPL; 18cb Prof. S.H.E. Kaufmann & Dr. J.R. Golecki/ SPL; 19cla SPL; 19tc Saturn Stills/ SPL; 19cr Eric Grave/ SPL; 19bc Alfred Pasieka/ SPL; 20cr Quest/ SPL; 21tr & tc Adam Hart-Davis/ SPL; 21bl Robert Harding Picture Library; 21br John Walmsley/ SPL; 22cr SPL; 23clb SPL; 23tr Doug Plummer/SPL; 24bl Andrew Syred/ SPL; 24cl CNRI/ SPL; 24br NIBSC/ SPL; 25tc Francis Leroy, Biocosmos/ SPL; 25cr Dr. P. Marazzi/ SPL; 25 bl John Freeman; 26tr Alfred Pasieka/ SPL; 26c CNRI/ SPL; 26bl J. L. Carson, Custom Medical Stock Photo/ SPL; 26cb Matt Meadows, Peter Arnold Inc./ SPL; 28bc Prof. S.H.E. Kaufmann & Dr J.R. Golecki/ SPL; 29crt Eye of Science/ SPL; 29br Robert Harding Picture Library; 30br CNRI/ SPL; 31bl Alfred Pasieka/ SPL; 31br Martyn Chillmaid/ Robert Harding Picture Library; 31br Prof. P. Motta/ Dept. of Anatomy/ University "La Sapienza", Rome/ SPL; 31 bc Eye of Science/ SPL; 35cl Manfred Kage/SPL; 35bc CNRI/ SPL; 35cr Eric Grave/ SPL; 36br The Stock Market; 37cl BSIP VEM/ SPL; 39cra CNRI/ SPL; 39tc Quellette & Theroux, Publiphoto Diffusion/ SPL; 39br Saturn Stills/ SPL; 40l Quest/ SPL; 40cb John Wildgoose/ Wellcome Medical Photographic Library; 41tc CNRI/ SPL; 41cr Laura Wickenden; 42r CNRI/ SPL; 42cb Biophoto Associates/ SPL; 42-3 J. C. Revy/ SPL; 44br Quest/ SPL; 45br John Wildgoose/ Wellcome Medical Photographic Library; 47bc Warren Anatomical Museum, Harvard Medical School, Boston; 49br Christopher Bissell/ Tony Stone Images; 50tr Laura Wickenden; 51tr Dr Robert Freidland/SPL; 51cr Andrew Sydenham; 52l Prof. P. Motta/ Dept. of Anatomy/ University "La Sapienza", Rome/ SPL; 52cr Omikron/ SPL; 52cb BSIP VEM/ SPL; 53cr Martin Dohrn/SPL; 53cl Biophoto Associates/ SPL; 53tr Prof. P. Motta/ Dept. of Anatomy/University "La Sapienza", Rome/ SPL; 54bl Kit Houghton/ SPL; 54bc Martin Dohrn/SPL; 55bl Astrid and Hans-Freider Michler/SPL; 55tl Manfred Kage/SPL; 55tc Will and Deni McIntyre/SPL; 56cl & cla Adam Hart-Davis/ SPL; 57cr Wellcome Dept. of Cognitive Neurology/ SPL; 57bl Omikron/ SPL; 57cl Kevin Harrison/ medipics; 58bl Wellcome Medical Photographic Library; 59tc Wellcome Dept. of Cognitive Neurology/ SPL; 59cr Prof. P. Motta/ Dept. of Anatomy/ University "La Sapienza", Rome/ SPL; 59br James King-Holmes/ SPL; 60tr Prof. P. Motta/ Dept. of Anatomy/ University "La Sapienza", Rome/ SPL; 60cr Biophoto Associates/ SPL; 61cr BSIP VEM/ SPL; 62l Science Pictures Ltd/ SPL; 62bc SPL; 62cr Biophoto Associates/ SPL; 62-3 Mugshots/ Ace Photo Agency; 63tl Simon Fraser/ SPL; 63cr Scott Camazine/ SPL; 63bl Petit Format/ Nestle/ SPL; 64bc Simon Fraser/ MRC Unit, Newcastle General Hospital/ SPL; 64br Ed Reschke, Peter Arnold Inc./ SPL; 64-65 SPL; 64tr Prof P. Motta/ Dept. of Anatomy/ University "La Sapienza", Rome/SPL; 65bl Prof. P. Motta, G. Macchiarelli, S.A. Nottola/ SPL; 65tl Biophoto Associates/ SPL 65ct Dr. Yorgos Nikas/ SPL; 65cl Prof. P. Motta/ A. Caggiati/ University "La Sapienza", Rome/SPL 66bl Dept. of Clinical Cytogenetics, Adenbrookes Hospital/SPL; 66-7 & 67c Biophoto Associates/ SPL; 67tr Dale Durfee/gettyone Stone; 67 br & bc Susanna Price; 68-9 Ken Edward/SPL; 69bc Plailly/Eurelios/SPL; 69tr Simon Fraser/ SPL; 70br Don Fawcett/ SPL; 71ct Dr. Yorgas Nikas/ SPL; 71cl Dr. Yorgas Nikas/ SPL; 71bl CC Studio/ SPL; 71tr Petit Format/ Nestle/ SPL; 71br James King-Holmes/ SPL; 71tl Bubbles/ Denise Hager; 72br Bubbles/ Angela Hampton; 72cb Mike Bluestone/ SPL; 73tl Petit Format/ Nestle/ SPL; 73tc Neil Bromhall/ Genesis Films/ SPL; 73br James Stevenson/ SPL; 73bl Petit Format/ Nestle/ SPL; 74–75 Laura Wickenden except: 74bl Bubbles/ Ian West; 74cl & c Scott Camazine/ SPL; 75br Digital Vision; 75tc Bubbles/ Loisjoy Thurston; 76bl Digital Vision; 76-7 Digital Vision; 77tr Digital Vision; 77br Rob Lewine/ The Stock Market; 78clt Scott Camazine/ SPL; 78cl SPL; 78clb BSIP VEM/ SPL; 78bl CNRI/ SPL; 78crt Geoff Tompkinson/ SPL; 78crtii Wellcome Dept. of Cognitive Neurology/SPL; 78crb CNRI/ SPL; 78crbii CNRI/ SPL; 78br Prof P. Motta/ A. Caggiati/ University "La Sapienza", Rome/SPL.